Inheritance and Resistance

Biblical Hermeneutics Rediscovered

The Series as the name suggests will focus on Biblical Hermeneutics, i.e., literary works concerned with methods of interpreting the Old and New Testaments of Bible via different stream of topics like Literature & Poetry, Indigenous Philosophizing, Ethical response towards Ecology, Health & Healing, Science & Technology, Feminist Theology, Sociological approach towards Human Rights, Law & Politics, Arts, History of Ideas, Ancient Civilizations, Cultural Contiguity, Religious Cosmologies & Mysticism, Appraisal of various Theologians, World Peace & Harmony, Global Capitalism, Network Marketing, Cybertheology, Population & Demographics, Epigraphic Studies, Contextualized Education, and many others. We welcome a Mss. on any topic/s mentioned, whether they are original works, scholarly monographs, collections of conference papers, revised dissertations, or translations of historical documents. Through the Series we, the Publishers, are striving to put forward published works that may help Institutions, Academic Bodies, Researchers, Scholars and the World at large in furthering their respective knowledge and understanding on the concerned subject. We welcome your comments on our efforts and further suggestions on how we can enshrine new ray of analysing & explaining the written Texts through our upcoming books.

Biblical Hermeneutics Rediscovered - 34

Inheritance and Resistance

Reclaiming Bible, Body, and Power

Mothy Varkey

Christian World Imprints

First Published in 2020 by

Christian World Imprints
Christian Publishing & Books from India
C-3, Wazirpur Industrial Area
Delhi-110052
cwidelhi2017@gmail.com
www.ChristianWorldImprints.com
Phone: +91 11 41526079

ISBN: 978-93-5148-467-7 (HB)
ISBN: 978-93-5148-468-4 (PB)

Printed in India.

Contents

Introduction

First and foremost, I thank God, the source of my being and in whom I exist, whose amazing grace, guided, and molded me all my life. This book is divided into **two sections.** This book is a compilation of essays that have appeared, either verbatim or edited into shorter versions, in various theological journals—NCCR, Religion and Society, and Bangalore Theological Forum etc.,—and books. A few articles are revised versions of papers presented at national and international seminars.

Section One comprises five essays which attempt to reclaim the intersectional relationship between body, power, and scripture. The first chapter—"Earth as Collective Inheritance"—argues that human beings are created in the 'green-image' of God (Genesis 2–3) and can thus become the agents of green ethics and green justice. "Power, Body, and Resistance" unpacks the counter imaginations of power as reflected in Matthew's Gospel. The third article, "'Cruciform Humanity' and Jesus' Miracles," examines M. M. Thomas' hermeneutical approach towards Jesus' miracles in Luke' Gospel. In the fourth essay, "Paul's Self-Description as 'Aborted Apostle,'" the focus is on Paul's resistance to dominant discourses on apostolicity confined to 1 Corinthians. The fifth essay—"The Melchizedek Tradition and Jesus' High Priesthood"—investigates the use of Melchizedek tradition in the Letter to the Hebrews from the vantage point of postcolonial biblical interpretation.

Section Two of this book consists of three essays. In "Ekklēsia of the Multitude," the Protestant talk of "justification by faith alone" is construed against the contemporary socio-political needs and ekklēsiological concerns than have been generally recognized. The second essay in this section—"Luther, Scripture, and Resistance"—unravels how Luther used his view of the scripture as a tool for his resistance movement against papacy and clericalism. It is reasoned in the final essay, "Mind-Body Dualism and Embodied Anthropology," that each of the explored bodily processes (speech, anatomy, and assistive technology) participates in a shared aim of self and other designation, which suggests the experience of self and world as non-dual.

My sincere thanks to *Christian World Imprints*, especially my friend **Sudhanshu Kanda**, for publishing this book. I am also grateful to Dr George Zachariah, Dr Vincent Rajkumar, Rev Dr David Joy, Rev Dr P G George and Fr Thomas Ninan for publishing a few of the essays in this book in their edited works.

Chapter 1

Earth as a Collective Inheritance
Towards a 'Green-image of God'

"Mother Earth still alive, in the imminence of your death,
may your soul rest in peace!
This song I inscribe in my heart today is a requiem to you (and to me)!
When tomorrow you lie benumbed
in the shadow of the enveloping dark poison-flower of death,
none will be left here, me either,
to mourn, to wet your dead lips with our tears!
Therefore, I inscribe this to you:
here is a wish, Mother Earth, not yet dead,
in the imminence of your death, may your soul rest in peace!"
(*A Requiem to Mother Earth*,
by Padma Shri O N V Kurup).

Lynn White's article entitled "The Historical Roots of our Ecologic Crisis" (1967), perhaps the most cited piece in the whole ecotheological debate, is still considered in academic circles not only as a watershed in religious thought regarding the environment, but also as a definitive indictment of christianity for crimes against nature.[1] It has stimulated examination of the relationship between religion, particularly christianity, and attitudes toward nature across the globe. In this highly provocative article, White maintained that as modern science and technology are products of western culture, and western culture has at its roots in christian attitudes and principles, christianity "bears a huge burden of guilt" for our current ecological crisis. However, White does not dismiss the christian tradition out of hand; he appeals to the figure of St. Francis as a positive model, a potential "patron saint for ecologists."[2]

In his analysis, White noted that the human capacity to wreak damage and destruction upon the environment grows out of western technological and scientific advances which occurred in a social context informed by the judeo-christian tradition. The overemphasis on anthropocentrism gives humans an unbridled permission to exploit 'nature' and transform it into 'culture'. White argued that within christian theology, "nature has no reason for existence… [but exist] to serve [humans]."

At the end of Genesis 1, the writer concludes, "God saw everything that had been made and indeed, it was very good" (Gen 1:31). This scripture also describes a special relationship that God has with humans through the *imago dei,* which asserts that human beings are created in the image and likeness of God. Following the Jewish tradition, it is argued that being made in the *imago dei* does not mean that God possesses human-like features, but rather that the statement is figurative language for God bestowing special honor unto humankind, which he did not confer unto the rest of creation. The human person in the image of God (Gen 1:26-28; 5:1-3; 9:6), like the image of a sovereign on a coin, is a representative and a regent who represent the sovereign in the midst of all other subjects where the sovereign is not directly and personally present. Thus, the

[1] Lynn White Jr., *Science* 155/3767 (March 1967), 1203-1207.

[2] Pope John Paul II named Francis the patron saint "of those who promote ecology" in 1979. Francis is the patron of those who cultivate ecological consciousness, but that means a lot more than being the patron of environmental educators. His example really points to a mystical or a spiritual vision for all of the creative world as brother and sister, as he describes in his Canticle of the Creatures.

human person is entrusted with 'dominion' (Gen 1:28; Ps 8:5–8).[3] According to this world view, White suggests, everything that exists in the natural world was 'planned' by God "explicitly for man's benefit and rule; no item in the physical creation had any purpose ...[but] serve man's purpose."

Genesis could be interpreted as providing a justification for exploitation of nature, without regard to the consequences of that exploitation. In Genesis, when God considers the creation of humans, God says, "Let us make humankind in our image, according to our likeness; and let them have dominion over the fish of the sea, and over the birds of the air, and over the cattle, and over all the wild animals of the earth, and over every creeping thing that creeps upon the earth" (Gen 1:26). White points explicitly to this 'monarchy' of humanity over the rest of creation as the culprit for a christian attitude that denigrates the importance of nature. For Leonard Boff, anthropocentrism is "the imperial and anti-ecological anthropology." Such an 'anthropocentric anthropology' creates, as rightly Sallie McFague argues, a "hegemonic human being." This human monarchy over the rest of creation seems implied in the christian doctrine of the *imago dei*, humans created in the image of God.

Needless to say, White's thesis touched off a firestorm of controversy. While White has had his defenders, many christians — including the former US Vice President Al Gore in his book, *Earth in the Balance: Ecology and Human Spirit* (1992)— have argued that White has missed the theological point contained in the creation stories of Genesis, where nature is depicted positively.[4] Yet,

---

[3] "God blessed them, and God said to them, "Be fruitful and multiply, and fill the earth and subdue it; and have *dominion* over the fish of the sea and over the birds of the air and over every living thing that moves upon the earth." (Gen 1:28 NRSV).

"Yet you have made them a little lower than God, and crowned them with glory and honour. You have given them *dominion* over the works of your hands; you have put all things under their feet, all sheep and oxen, and also the beasts of the field, the birds of the air, and the fish of the sea, whatever passes along the paths of the seas (Ps 8:5-9 NRSV).

[4] *Earth in Balance* explains the world's ecological predicament and describes a range of policies to deal with the most pressing problems. It includes a proposed

for many other christians, White's thesis clearly struck an important chord. The gradual evolution of an ecological consciousness within the church caused many to begin questioning traditional anthropocentric interpretations of scripture. Today, the nature of God, God's relationship to the world, humanity's place in the earth's complex and fragile life system, and the notion of the salvation of the world and not just of humans are a few of the issues open for re-examination and reinterpretation. This calls for 'green reading' of the *imago dei* in Genesis.

According to Walter Brueggemann, rightly so, the Old Testament does not portray human beings as autonomous. Brueggemann said that being made in God's image meant that humans were created to rule over creation "in the way that God ruled over creation." Creatively using power to invite, evoke, and permit was what made *homo sapiens* special and a reflection of God, because this is the way that God exercized God's power. God ruled as a servant-king, but not as a dictator-tyrant; so should the species made in God's image.[5] In the Old Testament, Brueggemann contends, human persons are understood as situated in the same transactional processes with the holiness of Yahweh as in Israel, so that in a very general way the character and destiny of human persons replicate and reiterate the character and destiny of Israel ("covenantal notions of personhood"). This transactional process causes a 'biblical understanding' of human persons to stand at a critical distance and as a critical protest against all modern notions of humanness that move in the direction of autonomy.

Human family, created in the 'image of God' (Gen 1:27), is integrally connected to God–creation continuum. The phrase *imago dei* basically refers to those characteristics of human beings that make communication with God possible and enable them to take up God-given responsibilities outlined in Gen 1:28. Process theologian Marjorie Suchocki asserted that being made in God's image meant that humans were created in interrelationship with all living things, just as God exists in relationship with all that is. Being consciously

---

'Global Marshall Plan' to address current ecological issues.

[5] Walter Brueggemann, *Genesis* (Atlanta: John Knox Press, 1982), 32.

in relationship with all life on earth—human and nonhuman—was what made *Homo sapiens* special and a reflection of God, because God intentionally and intimately relates to all that God has made. God exists in loving relationship with all living things in the creation; so should the species made in God's image.[6]

As the author and source of life, God shares not only his image but also his very life and glory with the created order (Psalms 19). The creation thus participates in the life of the creator. God is biologically present in the entire creation and, henceforth, God's family includes the whole cosmos. According to Philip Clayton, "every emergent level in the hierarchy of the reality expresses a different attribute of the divine nature: from the law-like regularity of the physical world, through striving and purposiveness of the biological order, to the conscious intentionality and rationality of mental experience."

God is not separated from the creation because it is in whom "we live and have our being" (Col 1:15–20), though God is certainly more than the creation as a whole. For Jürgen Moltmann, the relationship between God and the creation is analogous to the relation of human body and mind. The defence for such an understanding however does not compromise the ontological transcendence of God. The belief that the creation exists only through 'God's concurrence' is also endorsed here. God did create the universe, not 'outside' of God's self, but organically related to himself/herself.

It democratizes an ancient Near Eastern royal usage of image language; all human beings are created in the image of God, not just kings. The result is that all inter-human hierarchical understandings are set aside; all human beings irrespective of the station in life stand together as image of God. It rejects all essentialist notions of human personhood; thus human person is to be understood in relational and not essentialist ways. For Mark Brett, the democratizing tendency in Gen 1:26–38 can be seen as anti-monarchic.[7]

---

[6] Marjorie Suchocki, Public Lecture, Franklin College, Franklin, Indiana (May, 1989).

[7] Mark Brett, *Genesis: Procreation and Politics of Identity* (London and NY: Routledge, 2000), 28.

Moreover, the idea that humanity is made in the 'image of God' is actually not very dominant in the Old Testament as one would think. As David Horrell correctly observes, it is found primarily in the opening chapters of Genesis (Gen 1:26–27; 5:3; cf. Wisd 2:23). The other place on the Old Testament where a similar idea is expressed, linked with a strong statement about humanity's 'dominion' over the earth, is in Psalms 8:5–6 ("Thou hast made him a little lower than God, And dost crown him with glory and majesty! Thou dost make him to rule over the works of Thy hands; Thou hast put all things under his feet"). Keith Carley, an important contributor in the Earth Bible series, argues that this Psalm represents "an apology for human domination" which does not conform to the ecojustice principles.

"Image of God" is not self-contained, self-sufficient and static as if God is an asocial reality. In the triune Godhead, the divine flows into the other without subjugating and without being subjugated. It implies that the fullness of humanity is shared, participatory and reciprocal. Fr. Balas has identified two directions of the notion of participation" (*metousia*): 'vertical' and 'horizontal'. The vertical participation is between the human beings and the uncreated creator. On the other hand, the horizontal participation is found in each level of the created order.

In a homily on Beatitudes, the Cappadocian Father Gregory of Nyssa said: "image of God means participation in the very characteristics of God to be the perfection of all good, all beauty, all love, all wisdom and all power." It means humanity is ordained to participate in the divine and to be co-creators and co-workers on earth. All the mysteries of the created order are not meant to be known, unraveled and understood. This dialectic of continuity and discontinuity between the creation and the creator explains why humanity is an intrinsic part of the created order, and not at par with the creator.

According to Paulos Mar Gregorios, the discontinuity between God and the creation (*diastema*) is the ground of God's ontological transcendence and incomprehensibility. While the creator is self-emanant and thus is not dependent on the creation (Psalms 90:1–5), the creation is no being in itself. The creation emanates from God, subsists only by the will of God, and cannot exist by itself. Forbidden fruit in Genesis is the symbolic representation of this discontinuity (*diastemic* existence) and continuity ('created existence') between the creator and the creation. In no way does this prohibition diminish the glory of humanity, instead it takes the entire created order in due respect.

Unlike the first creation story (Gen 1:1–2:4a), the second creation story (Gen 2:4b-25) provides a somewhat green image of God. In the words of Brueggemann, Genesis 2–3 provides two images of God: *potter*, and *farmer/gardener*. God as a *potter* (Gen 2:7) does a "hands on" craft on the subject. It is often noted that the verb *form* (*ysr*) as it pertains to creation is not by dictum, but by actual engagement with the raw stuff out of which the object is formed. It underscores human dependence *on* the rest of the creation and not human domination *over* the earth.

According to George Zachariah, Genesis 2–3 would have emerged from an agrarian community. Zachariah argues that "the vision of humanity that emerged from a farming community––a community of ecological and social relations of solidarity and communion which is antithetical to the logic of an imperial exploitative system—is that of a dependent and responsible member of the ecosystem with the vocation to farmers."[8] This green image of a God with his hands in the dirt is remarkable; this is no naïve theology, but a statement about the depths to which God has entered into the life of the creation. God's very life is then breathed into human; something of God's own self becomes an integral part of human identity, enabling life to move from God out into the larger world.

God is also imaged as a *farmer/gardener*, placing two trees in this garden; they are associated with the life and death and human choices related thereto (Deut 30:15–20). Yahweh as *gardener* is often the subject of the verb *plant*. In Isa 5:1–2 in particular, the gardener-vinedresser is involved with the founding of the garden, and uses, attentiveness, and extravagance in creating the

---

[8] George Zachariah, *Gospel in a Groaning World: Climate Justice and Public Witness* (NCCI/CSS: Thiruvalla, 2012), 66. See also Claus Westermann, *Creation* (translated by John J. Scullion; London: SPCK, 1971), 81-82.

best possible vineyard ("Let me sing for my beloved my love-song concerning his vineyard: My beloved had a vineyard on a very fertile hill. He dug it and cleared it of stones, and planted it with choice vines; he built a watchtower in the midst of it, and hewed out a wine vat in it; he expected it to yield grapes, but it yielded wild grapes"—Isa 5:1-2 NRSV).

God created human beings to "till and keep" the creation (Gen 2:15). It means that God created humanity in such a way that they would take care of the creation, just as the creator would do. Humanity is made creator and hence they have not replaced the creator nor do they act on behalf of the creator, rather they are co-workers with the creator. Nevertheless, they do reflect the 'goodness' ('image') of God and participate in the creative activity of God. The understanding of human family as the participants in God's plan for the creation neither dishonors the sovereignty of God nor exalts the human family above the 'ordained limits'. Hence, the primary responsibility of human beings created in the "green-image of God" is ecological.

As with Zachariah, Mark Brett also persuasively stresses how the concerns of the words 'dominion' and 'rule' in Gen 1:28 ("Be fruitful and multiply, and fill the earth, and *subdue* it; and *rule over* the fish of the sea and *over* the birds of the sky, and over every living thing that moves on the earth") reflect the ancient agrarian setting. According to Brett, possessing the land and domesticating animals can be seen as essential aspects of sustaining human life in such a setting, and the 'dominion' over the animals may be seen primarily as related to real threats posed by wild animals and the desire to control or remove such threats to human wellbeing.[9]

Conclusion

Human beings created in the 'green-image' of God, who is depicted as *potter* and *farmer/gardener* in Genesis 2–3, despite its 'ambivalent legacies' to an environmental reading of the creation story, can become the green-ethical agents and can thus become the green subjects of history. In Boff's words, "the destiny of the whole earth

[9] Brett, *Genesis*, 28-29.

system can depend [to a great extent] on the [green-]ethical choices made by humanity." As 'green-ethical beings,' the agency of human beings can heal the wounded earth and preserve our mother earth—our collective inheritance.

Our 'green' reading of Genesis 1 certainly offers some ecotheological tools vital to an ecological theology or highlights contemporary ecojustice issues such as the essential goodness of the creation, the 'green-image of God', and the stewardship model of humanity's relation to the earth. More so, the democratization of 'the image of God' ("ant-monarchic image of God") subverts the understanding that humanity as a whole is called to "rule over" the creatures, which Brett defines as 'species supremacy.'[10] which lies at the root of ecological crisis. However, 'green reading' of the Bible does raise many hermeneutical issues. For example, the crucial 'dominion' passage in Gen 1:28 at least opens to a reading which supports a sense of the uniqueness of humanity and right to use the rest of the creation for its benefit. Interpretation of ambivalent texts like Genesis 1–3 raises ambiguity on how to deal constructively with their anti-ecological legacies. In other words, a consistent 'green' reading of the Bible or sustaining the view that Bible is 'green' by default is challenging.

---

[10] Brett, *Genesis*, 28.

Chapter 2

Power, Body, and Resistance
A Postcolonial Reading of Matthew 5:38-42

Introduction

Salman Rushdie, in his novel, *Shalimar the Clown*, realistically captures the reality of our world: "Our lives, our stories flowed into one another's, were no longer our own." As a colonial text, Bible, has been used to legitimize the continuous subjugation and silencing of the "visited." It essentialized the life-affirming stories/discourses of the colonized as "irrational" and "superstitious," and colonized even the psyche of the natives. But the Bible is also a text of resistance when it is read from the vantage point of postcolonial concerns. Postcolonial theory, therefore, is an attempt to interrogate the knowledge/power system of the colonizer and to expose the counter discourses and practices of the colonized/marginal communities for counter existence, self-representation and new subjectivity. This essay, consequently, is an attempt to understand the counter imaginations of power (unusual invitation to engage the colonizers) as reflected in Matthew's Gospel, with special reference to Matt 5:38-42.

Counter Imaginations of Power

The colonizers and the pharisees used 'master-narratives' (Matt 5:38, 43: "An eye for an eye and a tooth for a tooth" and "love your neighbour and hate your enemy") to control the consciousness of the people, to (mis)represent the natives and to legitimize their oppressive systems. Those who engage in such narratives for (mis) representing the 'other' will have the power over the objects of its construction.[1] The notion of power which these discourses assume is 'fixed" or 'located.'

Jesus initiated a ground-breaking 'counter epistemology' (Matt 5:39, 44: "But I say to you") to resist the inherent and repressive binarisms. This alternative discourse is a kind of 'textual cleansing'[2] of the 'manipulative myths' in the theological archives of orthodox pharisaism and their promulgated fixations like 'enemy', 'neighbor', 'good', 'evil', 'just', and 'unjust' because 'truth' is a construction which comes to being within the dominant discourses on the knowledge about the 'other'. Hence, the new imaginations interrogate the meaning(s) which have been 'locked' in the contest over the 'ownership of the meaning.'

The laws of reciprocity (Matt 5:38, 43) are replaced by a life-affirming counter discourse (Matt 5:39-47) which is committed to retrieve voices of the 'variations'/ 'marginals' and interrogate the 'facts' of the dominant discourses. Discourses construct the objects of its knowledge and 'produces reality'. Discourse(s) is the medium which constitutes power and through which it is exercized. The counter discourses, therefore, provide a new subjectivity, devoid of the 'scars'/imprints of colonialism.

Search for the 'Lost Body' as Redefining Power

The colonizers and the Pharisees 'locked' the Matthean community/ the colonized into their bodies. So, the body became the locus of all violations. But the Matthean community, having new imaginations

[1] Gerald West, "A Real Presence, Subsumed by Others: The Bible in Colonial and Postcolonial Contexts," *Semeia* 88 (2001), 203.

[2] R. S. Sugirtharajah, "Textual Cleansing: A Move from the Colonial to the Postcolonial Version," *Semeia* 76 (1996), 9.

of the body, acquired self-consciousness and attained to the dialectic of subject and object. The body, therefore, has become the object of consciousness. The physical movements or the counter discursive practices in Matt 5:39-42 are the language of the revitalized physicality. These practices can reconstruct the 'lost body' of the colonized from the displaced/disembodied subject inflicted by the colonizer's pornographic gaze. For the reason that discursive practices form the bodies/objects, they are not external to these practices.

Body as a Site of Power/Resistance

Discourses can define, classify, categorize and form human beings. So the human body is the "inscribed surface of events" and the locus of 'dissociated self.' Freedom lies in the power to identify the 'genealogy' of the discursive formation. Foucault's discourse on body omitted the 'performative fact:' the body also moves. Postcolonial theory becomes liberative at this juncture. It pays attention to how the colonizers construct the body of the colonized as an inscribed object of knowledge. The colonial regimes target body, because it has the ability to affect an unpredictable threat to a system for it is capable of being 'self-marked' and 'self-represented.' Hence, the body is in no way an inactive/silent object upon which the colonial powers are played out. The body is thus the site of resistance/power.

The body's ability to move, reveal itself and even 'fracture' oppressive modes and social relations provide the site for "counter-strategic reinscription." It contests its essentialization and (mis) representation by the colonial discourses. This involves not just verbal/textual counter discourses but a performative/ 'theatrical' reviewing of the body and its 'signifying practices.' Matt 5:38-42 offers counter social practices to recover the colonized/ 'lost' body and subjectivity.

'Dancing Body' as New Body Language of Power

The colonizer's abuse and physical harm (Matt 5:39b: "if any one strikes you on the right cheek") and the demand to carry the luggage (Matt 5:41: "if any one forces you to go one mile") express the experiences of oppression. "Turning the other" cheek and "going two miles" are the non-verbal/non-violent forms of self-representation and positioning. It unveils the ability of the body to counter the predatory inscriptions on the body. By surprising the oppressor, the oppressed cross the zones of 'fixity' and 'perpiherality.' Both these 'provocative invitations' resist 'thingification'/objectification. They define and dictate the terms of relationship. This 'political activity' of the 'lost' body shows that the power is not 'located'/ 'fixed' in the colonized, rather it is 'diffused'. Therefore, the 'dancing'/moving body, hitherto 'locked', is a new body language of power.

'Reframing Body' as Liberative Praxis of Power

The ways in which the body is framed by/within the gaze determine how and what it can mean. The gaze establishes the loci of authority. The civilizing intent of clothing is a colonial representation. Colonial logic of 'clothing' is a marker to differentiate the 'civilized' and the 'savage'. Standing 'naked' in front of the oppressor (v.40) can invest the Matthean community/colonized with more varied and liberative viewing frames. This practice exposes the inherent cruelty of the system which the colonizer represents. So 'nakedness' affirms the worth of the 'derogated body' and escapes the 'gaze' of the colonizer which keeps the colonized in subservience and surveillance. It is a forceful invitation for the colonizer to get ashamed. The 'looking relations' therefore becomes the site of resistance. It challenges the 'pornographic gaze' of the colonizer and subverts the subjectivity that colonialism has assigned to the colonized subject.

'Metamorphic Body', Split Subjectivity, and Power

The counter practices in Matt 5:39-42 reflect the potential of the body for transformation/metamorphosis. There is no binarism between the oppressor and the oppressed. So, the colonized self is not a completed self or essential self. Consequently, the colonized self 'slides' ambivalently between 'affiliation' and 'disruption.' It will result in the creation of ambivalent/split subjects. It locates a 'slippage'/'fracture' in the 'prediction'/certainty of the colonial discourse regarding the behavior of the colonized objects. Split subjectivity removes both the colonizer and the colonized from their assigned positions. Instead of being 'fixed', both subject positions are dislocated. Foregrounding this moving and metamorphic capacity of the body is an active strategy for parading resistance.

New Subjectivity as 'Children of God'

Colonial discourses represent the colonized as a 'fixed' social reality that can be known. This negativity is a discursive feature that has been employed in the textualization of the colonized. The whole purpose of colonial discourses is to interpret the colonized as 'anonymous collectivity' and to produce subdued subjectivity. It is probable since the subject is the effect of discourses. There is no stereotyped *ousia* or *esse*, only constructions or 'discursive formations'. So, framing a new subjectivity, through counter social practices and discourse, is not impossible.

Human beings are not eternally and essentially constructed. So no one is ontologically 'evil' or 'good'. In other words, identity is not essence; rather it is a construction. Matthew, therefore, omits the definite article for 'good' and 'evil' (v.45). It is only a representation by the 'good'. It strategically essentializes the 'other'/ 'variant' as enemy. It legitimizes the colonial logic of 'cause and effect'. These 'fixed zones' or binary opposites, 'center' and 'margin;' 'inside' and 'outside;' 'good' and 'bad;' 'neighbor' and 'enemy;' 'just' and 'unjust'(v.43) etc., eliminate the differences. Such 'morphological' classifications will validate 'genctical inferiority' and 'marginality.' These 'regimes of truth' prevail through social practices and institutions like race and gender. Attitude towards the gentiles by the pharisees and the Matthean community must be analyzed in this context.

The politics of representation is being interrogated in vv. 43-45. The biologically constituted notions, 'good', 'evil', 'enemy' and 'neighbor', are questioned by counter imaginations and discourses pertaining to the love of God. The laws of reciprocity are being repudiated in v. 43. The bottom line is that using the colonial notion of power for countering the colonizers is suicidal because the Matthean community is only a marginal community. It is not going to (re)frame their subjectivity either.

For the pharisees and the Romans, 'neighbor' means those who subscribe to their discourses and logic. All the 'others' were essentialized as 'enemies'/'heretics'. The gentiles were stigmatized as 'evil' by the so called 'good.' But the sun rises on 'good' and 'evil'/'heretic' and God showers rain on the 'just' and the 'unjust.' 'Love' and 'pray' denote the counter social practices. Those who practise these counter discourses become the 'children of God' (v. 40). Here the processes of 'becoming' challenge 'fixity' and 'essentialism.' So for postcolonialists, the subjectivity is not given/static, rather it is an emerging/forming/framing subjectivity.

The community of the 'children of God', having divine subjectivity, participates in the all-inclusive love of God. The knowledge about the inclusive love of God is the key instrument of power in this sphere. They (re)locate and (re)imagine their position in the world. They (re)position themselves in subject position. Their practices are different from the hegemonic practices of colonialism (vv. 46-47). The counter practices/imaginations of power of the 'children of God' subvert gender and race. So, the institution called discipleship operates on the community/counter logic called 'greater righteousness.' For them, the new body languages/gestures are a political activity which would (re)frame a new social body. This liberative act of subjectivity formation is the challenge of the community of disciples.

New Epistemology of Power of the Children of God

There is no essential binarism between 'superior' and 'inferior'. Hence, the 'fixed' zones of dalits and women are only social constructions. The dalits and women are not genetically second best. Postcolonialism, thus, interrogates the politics of representation. Over and against the binarism, postcolonialism promises the possibility of a new subjectivity as the children of God. The all-inclusive love of God is the logic of this discourse. This is possible for all creation irrespective of the manipulative binary markings. This will challenge all the gender and caste discriminations.

The Matthean community, a marginal community, had to face the predatory rule of Roman colonialism and the threat from pharisees. Both the Romans and the pharisees constructed the image of the Matthean community/ 'other' as 'heretic'/'variant' and 'fixed' them in zones of marginality. The colonization of the life world was only an overt expression of the oppression and exploitation. They had even captivated the psyche of the colonized through repressive myths/discourses and discursive practices. It is in this context that the Matthean community initiated counter discourses and new social practices to (re)present and (re)frame the subjectivity.

The Matthean community had identified the liberative potential of the body for nonviolent resistance. Body is the most 'malleable and resonant' vehicle for subverting and interrogating/problematizing the representation/positioning and surveillance/'anatomizing gaze' that the 'civilized'/male/'superior' has inflicted on the 'savage'/female/'inferior'. This will distinguish the bodies of the 'marginals' like women and dalits not only as the colonies of aggression and representation, but also as sites of new discourses of resistance/power and self-worth. This is the 'politics of difference' envisaging a 'differentiated subjectivity' through counter discourses and discursive social practices.

Body and Power: Towards a Postcolonial Dalit/Feminist Reconfigurations

As the dalits and women live under the far-reaching pressures of globalization and market forces in the new colonial dispensation, how do they read the text, Bible, as a text of resistance? How do their stories, myths and memories inscribed on the body impel them for a new epistemology of power? How can a colonial text like the Bible function as a text of resistance?

The very understanding that the biblical narratives are evolved from the colonial experience of the people is in itself liberative for the dalits and women. It enables them to interrogate the colonial logic of 'cause and effect' and the ways in which they were (mis) represented and strategically essentialized. It takes into consideration the multiple realities of 'perpiherality' and the conspiracy of 'silence.' It unchains their bodies and fosters the voicing of previously unheard cries. It also helps to realize that a new meaning(s) is constructed when their 'derogated'/colonized bodies turn out to be the sites of a 'discursive engagement' with the text. They interrogate the casteist and gender constructions and consider them as the 'locations'/ context of theologizing.

The totalizing colonial discourses/meta narratives, constructed knowledge about the colonized/'other' in the form of myths. They have represented natives as incapable, immature and evil to legitimize and carry on a system of dominion. So also, over the years, the dalits and women have been essentialized and framed as 'variants', 'superstitious', 'untouchable', 'ugly', 'inferior' etc. This biological stereotyping assumed the institutional forms of casteism and patriarchy. In order to (re)present and (re)frame the image of the dalits and women, initiating new discourses and practices are of vital importance because discourses form the objects of its knowledge. In other words, the subject is the effect of discourses. It is at this point that the 'unvisited' body that mediated experiences of multiple forms of subjugation and violence become the 'archives' of liberative discourses.

Through the centuries, the bodies of the dalits and women have become the 'inscribed surface of events' and the site of 'dissociated self'. They have been 'locked' in their bodies. It means that the body is the site of all violations. The exponents of casteism and patriarchy were scared of the liberative potential of the body. This is, precisely, because the body has the ability to surprise the oppressor. Postcolonialism celebrates the potential of the body to make spur-of-the-moment threat. The 'capillary' form of power is the reason for this body politics. It assumes that the body moves, and that too ambivalently. It revises the 'pornographic gaze' of the oppressor, and frequently 'fractures' it. Re-politicization of body escapes the repressive surveillance of the oppressor. It is in this space, that the liberation of the dalits and women lies.

The nonviolent physical movements of the body are the counter practices. These provocations are invitations for an unusual form of resistance and 'self-marking.' All relations of power are 'force relations' and where there is power, there is resistance. Like power, resistance also has multiple points. So, it is not impossible to engage in the acts of resistance. The nonviolent discursive practices of resistance release new vistas of liberation for dalits and women.

This is very important for their subjectivity formation as discursive practices form the objects; they do not exist outside of these practices.

Dalits and women have been strategically taught by the manipulative myths of 'cause and effect' that their essence is unchangeable. It means that their subjectivity is 'fixed.' But postcolonial theory has shown that identity is not essence; rather a construction. Subjectivity is not essentially and eternally given. This knowledge itself is liberation; and hence it is power. This counter discourse of power helps the 'variants' like dalits and women to reject all casteist and patriarchal inscriptions on their bodies. This is possible by initiating new discourse and participating in discursive struggles of liberation.

Thus far, the liberation struggles of dalits and women operated on Marxian logic of dialectical materialism. We know from the collapse of such movements that, unless they address the cultural and psychological effects of subjugation, they cannot produce enduring results. Postcolonialism locates itself distinctively at this point. It takes into consideration the socio-economic relations of the society as internal conditions of power. Postcolonial theory, therefore, can facilitate the struggles of dalits and women since it avows justice in all its dimensions.

Conclusion

"No one colonizes innocently," as Aime Cesaire put it long ago, is one of the most decisive and abiding rationales of postcolonialism. It presumes that nobody interferes in other people's matters if it were not for some political and economic interests. Postcolonialism investigates the 'genealogy' of such insatiable intentions and the ensuing atrocities. Postcolonial biblical interpretation exceedingly fits into this theoretical landscape. The fact that the biblical narratives, too, evolved from the formerly colonized communities, underscores the historical experiences/conditions of colonialism. It seeks to position colonialism at the core of the biblical interpretation and interrogates colonial logic ingrained in the text/Bible and its readings. It engages with the cultural and textual articulations and representations of the communities affected by colonialism and neo-colonialism.

Unlike the totalizing forms of colonial discourses, postcolonial reading practices expose/challenge the power dynamics, mutually constitutive relationship *entre* knowledge and power, that were used to oppress the natives/colonized. It analyses the strategies by which the colonizers discursively constructed the image of the colonized and the ways in which the colonized made use of, and went beyond those strategies for 'self-marking' and continued existence. The struggle of the Matthean community for self-positioning, (re)presentation and new subjectivity is examined in this theoretical framework.

Roman colonial powers controlled and conditioned the Matthean community, with the help of formative Judaism, through political invasion, cartography, subservience, (mis)representation, surveillance and strategic essentialization. The construction of 'master-myths' ('truth') concerning the 'other'/colonized, 'infant,' 'irrational', 'savage', 'inherently incapacitated' etc., was their *le plus important* stratagem. These 'fixities' are inscribed or 'mapped across the bodies' of the 'visited' in and through discourses and disciplinary regimes. The exponents of colonialism assert that the 'occupied' are incompetent of managing power. Therefore they must be ruled/ represented by the 'civilized.' These stereotypical constructions/ portrayals are used as 'ideological tools'/ 'scared canopy' to rationalize colonialism.

It was a systemic cultural infiltration and domination. The cultural, rational and psychological domination was more destructive. Though being in the fold of Judaism, the Matthean community had created an all-inclusive institution, *ekklēsia*, and fêted Jesus' counter discourses of power and discursive social practices as reflected in Matthew 5:38-48. They had also celebrated Jesus' discourse on the liberative and moving potential of the body. Body is not inactive/passive/silent/uni-dimensional object; rather it has the capacity to move, cover up, reveal itself and effect an unpredictable threat to a system for it is capable of self-positioning. In other words, body is the site of resistance and power.

The counter discourse and social practices/offensive invitations ('turn', 'go', 'nakedness' etc.,) subvert the colonial logic and binary markings. It envisages a counter epistemology of power and a new subjectivity. Discourses and discursive practices can form the objects of its knowledge. It unravels the prospect for a 'process of becoming.' This process of becoming interrogates the notion of essential self, stereotyped *esse* and all kinds of myths which legitimize genetical inferiority and biological dependence. 'Perfection' is the acme of this process and the new subjectivity is called the 'children of God'. It is based on the all-embracing love of God.

The discursively fabricated binary markers of 'identity'/ subjectivity, race and gender are not timeless directives or eternally given, rather historical and cultural constructions. It tactically classifies human beings into physically and genetically distinct groups. It means humanity is divided into 'fixed' natural quintessence. Colonialism, patriarchy and casteism are imbued with identical thrust to draw a binary distinction between 'superior' and 'inferior.' In these institutions, the oppressed is denied full humanity and sense of subjectivity.

To sum up, postcolonial reading practice(s) needs to reflect on the multiple realities/nuances of subjugation. They challenge the casteist and gender constructions and consider them as discursive formations. It shows that caste and gender are 'mapped across the body' by way of (mis)representation, punitive regulations and social practices. The view of 'truth as mapped, constructed and negotiated' provides the *raison d'être* for counter discourses and collective practices. Postcolonial epistemology of power will facilitate the 'variants'/'marginals', dalits and women to distinguish their 'shift ing'/'sliding'/'multivalent' bodies not only as sites of violence and (mis)representation, but also as sites of 'self-marking,' resistance and power.

Chapter 3

'Cruciform Humanity' and Jesus' Miracles

Φθείρουσιν ἤθη χρηστὰ ὁμιλίαι κακαί (1 Cor 15:33)
[Bad ***homilies/conversations*** corrupt good morals]

Introduction

M. M. Thomas made an exceptional and enduring contribution to contextual biblical hermeneutics. As it seems to be in the case of the Latin American/Hispanic theologians and activists, Asian theologians, in general, were more into doing theology in their socio-political context. This caused, as T. M. Philip rightly notes in his general preface to Thomas' commentary on Luke's Gospel, which is the primary resource for this study, a 'dearth' in "biblical exegesis on solid contextual-theological foundation."[1]

Therefore, Thomas took up the daunting undertaking to write bible commentaries in his vernacular–Malayalam. Though Thomas' intention was *not* to provide a 'scientific exegesis' on the books of the

[1] M. M. Thomas, *Jesus God's Anointed (Luke 1–9)* (Translated by T. M. Philip; CTBC 8; Thiruvalla: CSS & BTTBPSA, 2007), 6.

Bible through his unique experiment, his commentaries, however, to a great extent, recompensed the 'drought' of biblical hermeneutics in the context of the struggles for justice and questions raised by pluralism in Asia in general, and in India in particular. At the same time, Thomas also aimed at the theological (re)orientation and (trans) formation of the laity across denominational boundaries. His ecumenical perspective/s have either 'redrawn' or 'blurred' the denominational and 'traditional' dogmatic margins which act both as a boundary marker or as an identity marker that 'isolates' a faith community from the rest of the human community. This essay attempts to unpack M M Thomas' hermeneutical approach towards Jesus' miracles in Luke's Gospel.

Miracles in Luke's Gospel

As with any other outstanding Lukan commentators, Thomas also correctly deciphers and unravels the theological characteristics of Luke's Gospel. According to Thomas, the Lukan understanding of the 'liberation *dharma*' of Jesus is holistic.[2] And, therefore, the liberation that God brings in through the person of Jesus and his salvific ministry, which includes his words and deeds, cannot be just limited to "justice to the oppressed and justification of the sinner."[3] Instead, Thomas correctly argues, Jesus' saving mission in Luke includes "possession by the evil spirit, disease, death–all these are satanic forces that destroy the human person."[4] In Thomas' opinion, Luke's understanding of satan also means the forces that are responsible for poverty, sin, death, oppression, disease;[5] satanic forces are the systemic and structural agencies that dehumanize people and communities. It is at this juncture that Thomas deviates from liberation theology according to which the liberation which God offers in Jesus is liberation from social injustice and oppression.[6]

---

[2] Thomas, *Jesus God's Anointed*, 23.

[3] Thomas, *Jesus God's Anointed*, 23.

[4] Thomas *Jesus God's Anointed*, 23.

[5] Thomas *Jesus God's Anointed*, 23–24.

[6] Thomas, *Jesus God's Anointed*, 20.

In contrast, Thomas persuasively contends that "Jesus liberated humanity not only from social injustice but also from sin and death."[7]

In other words, for Luke, God in Jesus liberates his people from the clutches of all the satanic forces of dehumanization. If so, Jesus' saving activity imagines a new/alternative world or a system, which, for Luke, is the kingdom of God, as in Mark, where dehumanized people are rehumanized according to the image of God as manifested in Jesus. Jesus embodies this reimagined humanity, which, for Thomas, is the new humanity. Thus Thomas closely associates salvation and humanization. For Luke, as Thomas aptly interprets, miracles are more than mere healing activity as they signal the arrival of the kingdom of God in Jesus where rehumanized humanity is envisaged.[8] While Moses liberated the people of Israel from the brickyards of Pharaoh and David from the Philistines, Jesus liberates the entire humanity, and hence the name: Christ the savior. Against this larger theological setting, Thomas interprets Luke's understanding of Jesus' miracles.

The community behind Luke's Gospel might have used the tradition about Jesus' healing of the man with the uncleaned spirit at Capernaum (Luke 4:31–37) and the healing of the mute (Luke 11:14–26).[9] Demon possession—which, in Thomas' observation, came in to Judaism through Babylon and Persia—was considered as centers of evil power.[10] Such demonic powers corrode the humanity of people. Jesus has the divine power to rehumanize the possessed which he exercizes by exorcising those who were possessed. He also rebukes the fever of Simon's mother-in-law (Luke 4:40). Luke thus shows Jesus' authority over demons and evil spirits manifested in his healing as in of his teaching. This stands in historical, theological and soteriological continuity with the Jewish understanding that the Messiah will sanctify the world by defeating the satanic/demonic

---

[7] Thomas, *Jesus God's Anointed*, 20.

[8] Thomas, *Jesus God's Anointed*, 23.

[9] M. M. Thomas, *In Jesus the Kingdom of God is Near (Luke 9–19)* (Translated by T. M. Philip; CTBC 9; Tiruvalla: CSS & BTTBPSA, 2007), 62–63.

[10] Thomas, *Jesus God's Anointed*, 87.

powers and thus restore humanity.[11] Thomas clearly interprets the miracles of Jesus in Luke's Gospel as indicative of the arrival of kingdom of God as prophesied by the Jewish prophets, and of his christological authority as the "Son of God" (Luke 4:41) and "the Holy One of God" (Luke 4:34). For Thomas, healing of the demon possessed man is salvation of his humanity.[12]

Thomas notes that the cleansing of the leprosy affected person in Luke 5:12–16 (cf. Matt 8:1–4; Mark 1:40–45) reveals not just Jesus' power to heal but also his politics of compassion. In the Old Testament, leprosy was foremost a social disease and those inflicted with the disease were regarded as religiously and ceremoniously 'unclean' and hence separated from the rest of the community (Lev 13–14).[13] But, Jesus 'breaks' some of the aspects of the law of Moses which dehumanizes the leprosy affected person by touching his/her 'impure body.' In doing so, Jesus himself becomes unclean. More importantly, according to Thomas, the modern translations use the word 'be healed' instead of 'be clean' which is more telling. He argues, "Jesus dissociated leprosy from its cultic connotation (clean/unclean) and handled it as a physical disease."[14] Thomas uses this miracle to address caste system in India and the untouchability associated with it which treats 'bodies' of the dalits as 'impure.'[15] He challenges such dehumanizing religious/cultic laws on the basis of the gospel of the kingdom of God which consider all human as clean in Jesus which is the basis of 'universal human fraternity.'[16] More importantly, Thomas argues for a secular social space which is thoroughly humanized and free from dehumanizing cultic laws and religious dogmas.

Luke uses the tradition regarding the healing of the paralytic (Luke 5:17–26; cf. Matt 9:2–8; Mark 2:1–12) by forgiving his sins as a justification for the early church's proclamation of forgiveness

[11] Thomas, *Jesus God's Anointed*, 89.

[12] Thomas *Jesus God's Anointed*, 89.

[13] Thomas, *Jesus God's Anointed*, 90.

[14] Thomas, *Jesus God's Anointed*, 90.

[15] Thomas, *Jesus God's Anointed*, 90–91.

[16] Thomas, *Jesus God's Anointed*, 90–91.

of sins in the name of Jesus (Acts 2:38).[17] For Thomas, paralysis could possibly be a psycho-somatic disease because the "deep guilt in human conscience can affect body and mind."[18] This explains why Luke, as in Mark and Matthew, believes that healing requires forgiveness of sins, which sits well with the close relation between sin and sickness in Judaism (Exod 20:5; Lev 26:14–16; Deut 28:21–22; 2 Chr 21:15, 18–19; Ps 103:3; 4Q510; 1Qap Gen 20:16–29). Thomas is of the view that had the paralytic or the people who brought him responded negatively, Jesus would not have been able to heal him; "without human cooperation it can be said that Jesus is powerless."[19] In other words, 'God's self-limitation' as exemplified in Jesus indicates the extent of human freedom.[20] If miracles signal rehumanization of humanity in Jesus, as we have seen above, then, as Thomas would possibly say, humanization is possible only when human community exercizes its God given freedom in such a way that it amounts to delimit God's self-imposed limitation. Therefore, salvation means delimiting God's assumed limits. This calls for a (new) politics of humanization and compassion as embodied in Jesus which invites human community to participate in it and thus become "political saints."

In the story of the healing of a man with a withered hand (Luke 6:6–11),[21] a crippled woman (Luke 13:10–17),[22] and a man with dropsy (Luke 14:1–6),[23] for Thomas, Luke has Jesus invite his audience to celebrate sabbath as an act of love.[24] Thomas rather cogently argues that sabbath and all other religious events are to be observed in such a way that they liberate people from all sorts of dehumanizing forces. As Thomas rightly observes, Luke has Jesus insist that sabbath being "a sign of final liberation" should be subject

[17] Thomas, *Jesus God's Anointed*, 91.

[18] Thomas, *Jesus God's Anointed*, 91–92.

[19] Thomas, *Jesus God's Anointed*, 92, 126

[20] Thomas, *Jesus God's Anointed*, 92.

[21] Thomas, *Jesus God's Anointed*, 97.

[22] Thomas, *In Jesus the Kingdom of God is Near*, 90–91.

[23] Thomas, *In Jesus the Kingdom of God is Near*, 97–98

[24] Thomas, *Jesus God's Anointed*, 97.

to the liberative growth of humanity and the celebration of life and mercy. Humanization means doing good and saving life. Therefore, Thomas contends, Lukan Jesus at times, as in Mark and Matthew, 'breaks' the Law not only to redeem the true sense of the sabbath observance but also to uphold the dignity of humanity (Luke 6:1–11; 13:10–14).[25] More importantly, such observance actualizes itself as it entails salvation and humanization which is the ultimate purpose of any religious practice.

As with the healing of the paralytic in 5:17–26, Lukan community retells the story of the gentile centurion at Capernaum as recorded in 7:1–10[26] and the centurion at the foot of the cross in 23:47[27] not only to justify welcoming gentiles into its fold but also as a response to the criticisms within the community against it.[28] In Thomas' view, the gentile centurion would have been a part of the worship at the synagogue given the testimony of the Jewish leaders about the centurion ("He is worthy to have you do this for him, for he loves our nation, and he built us our synagogue"—Luke 7:4–5).[29] While the Jewish leaders' testimony is based on the favors the centurion did for their community, the centurion's self-understanding transcends the communal approach of the Jewish leader as it is based on seeing who Jesus is.[30] This is the kind of humanization that transcends the humanly erected walls of 'purity' that Jesus invites the entire humanity into. It also shows the astounding outbreaking of the kingdom of God into the world in Jesus. Thomas thus shows how Luke employs Jesus traditions to address the rampant and potential historical and theological challenges of his community. This calls for not only the possibility of but also the rationale for contextualizing the stories of Jesus and the faith traditions associated with it.

---

[25] Thomas, *In Jesus the Kingdom of God is Near*, 97–98.

[26] Thomas, *Jesus God's Anointed*, 110.

[27] M. M. Thomas, *Crucified Jesus the Lord of the World (Luke 19–24)* (Translated by T. M. Philip; CTBC 10; Tiruvalla: CSS & BTTBPSA, 2008), 103-104.

[28] Thomas, *Jesus God's Anointed*, 109.

[29] Thomas, *Jesus God's Anointed*, 110.

[30] Thomas, *Jesus God's Anointed*, 111.

Lukan community's contextual theologizing is further reflected in the raising of a widow's son at Nain in Luke 7:11–17 and Jairus' daughter in 8:40–56.[31] While these stories were used to counter allegations against the teaching of the Lukan community concerning Jesus' divine authority to raise the dead, Luke has also used them to justify and validate the preaching of his community. The raising of the dead is a sign of God visiting the earth;[32] God's visitation has become a historical reality in Jesus. According to Thomas, it caused fear among humans because of the "awareness of God's transcendent nearness."[33] That is to say, it is "God's transcendent nearness" that makes salvation from death and humanisation possible.

Jesus' healing of a demon possessed man in Luke 8:26–39 is another instance of how Lukan community uses Jesus' encounter with the gentiles to legitimize the inclusion of the gentiles to his community, as elsewhere in Luke 7:1–10 and 23:47.[34] However, Thomas takes these stories only as indications of universality given that Jesus removes the ethnic barriers only after his resurrection, as in Matt 28:19–20.[35] As we have seen earlier (Luke 4:31–37), in Thomas' opinion, demons dehumanize and alienate the self by disintegrating it.[36] For Thomas, disintegration means contradictions within the self which is an offshoot of the onslaught of the fall described in Genesis 3.[37] Jesus rehumanizes the disintegrated self of the demon possessed by integrating it; salvation and humanization would also mean integration of self and "unification of personhood" as manifested in Jesus.[38] New humanity which God offers in Jesus therefore means integrated self and unified person.

According to Thomas, Jesus' miracles in no way quash the public health service and church's ministry of healing through

---

[31] Thomas, *Jesus God's Anointed*, 110–111, 126–127

[32] Thomas, *Jesus God's Anointed*, 111, 126–127.

[33] Thomas, *Jesus God's Anointed*, 111.

[34] Thomas, *Jesus God's Anointed*, 125.

[35] Thomas, *Jesus God's Anointed*, 125.

[36] Thomas, *Jesus God's Anointed*, 125–126.

[37] Thomas, *Jesus God's Anointed*, 126.

[38] Thomas, *Jesus God's Anointed*, 126.

medical mission services because "Jesus can heal through physicians as well as without them."[39] This position is exemplified in the account of Jesus' healing of a woman who had suffered from severe bleeding for twelve years (Luke 8:43–48). For Thomas, prayers, though they are indeed a spiritual source of healing, are a not a substitute for medical services. In its place, as Thomas rightly puts it, churches should "undertake prayer services along with medical services."[40] He also argues that it is the political responsibility of the church to resist state's gradual withdrawal from public health services and neo-liberal policy to privatize the heath sector.[41] Thomas also maintains that churches should continue to set up (new) hospitals to offer heath care to the poor communities.[42]

In Luke's Gospel, Thomas notes, there is no dichotomy between the 'spiritual' and 'physical' aspects of the salvation; instead, both are "closely interrelated in the message of the kingdom."[43] But, this is not something very unique to Luke; it is continuous with the understanding of the salvation/liberation which God offers in the Old Testament. The God who saves his people from their sins and from Pharaoh is also the one who saves Israelites from perishing from hunger by feeding them in the desert with manna and prepares a banquet for them (Exod 16).[44] While the disciples are terrified by the huge size of the multitude and the "limited possibilities of the existing situation," Jesus invites them to imagine "the new possibilities ingrained in the Kingdom of God"—"You give them something to eat" (Luke 9:13). Thomas contextualizes Jesus' demand to the original band of apostles as in Luke 9:13 as a perpetual instruction and reminder to the churches in India that encounter millions

[39] Thomas, *Jesus God's Anointed*, 126.

[40] Thomas, *Jesus God's Anointed*, 127.

[41] Thomas, *Jesus God's Anointed*, 127.

[42] Thomas, *Jesus God's Anointed*, 127; M. M. Thomas, *The Church's Mission and Post-Modernism: Collection of Essays and Talk 1992–1996* (Tiruvalla and Delhi: CSS and ISPCK, 1996), 42–43.

[43] Thomas, *Jesus God's Anointed*, 131.

[44] Thomas, *Jesus God's Anointed*, 131.

who suffer abject poverty.[45] For Thomas, the miracle of feeding the multitude is not just an event to be romanticized and celebrated eternally as it testifies Jesus' divine authority and his compassion but is a call to observe Jesus' feeding of the hungry as a mission directive to engage in the politics of compassion revealed in Jesus.

The politics of compassion is further evident in Luke 9:37–43 where Jesus heals a demon possessed boy. Thomas highlights the two contrasting pictures of humanity in the narrative: the glory of humanity on the mount of transfiguration and the 'disfigured' humanity at the valley. To contextualize the miracle, Thomas uses Paul Lehman's concept of 'transfiguration of politics' which to a great extent informs liberation theology developed in Latin America and elsewhere. In Thomas' appraisal, the Indian church seeking transformation in the community must contextualize the meaning of the glory of humanity revealed in Jesus on the mount of transfiguration rather than being carried away by the dogmatic and creedal shades of the event. Transfiguration is not to be understood as a closed and one-off event, instead it must flow into the 'valley' where humanity is 'disfigured' and thereby rehumanize the dehumanized. Transformation must be an ongoing experience both on the mountain and in the valley. By meeting the human needs in the 'visible' and 'invisible' 'valleys' of the Indian society where 'disfiguration' of humanity is rampant, church transforms not only the 'disfigured' humanity but also the very 'valley' itself. Furthermore, church 'transfigures' herself not by locating herself on the mountain but at the 'disfigured valley.' For Thomas, Jesus' healing of the 'disfigured' and dehumanized boy in the valley redefines and revisits the very meaning of the 'figure' of the church and the 'transfiguration' she needs to undertake.

Thomas argues that Luke's understanding of salvation through miracles in Luke 17:11–19, where Jesus' healing of ten leprosy affected persons is recorded, is integral and holistic: salvation includes both forgiveness of sins and healing of sickness.[46] Salvation is God's free gift as it is an expression of God's grace and therefore it elicits gratitude. It is gratitude that leads humans from "self-

[45] Thomas, *Jesus God's Anointed*, 131.

[46] Thomas, *In Jesus the Kingdom of God is Near*, 115–116.

centred life to a God-centred life."[47] For Thomas, Luke has Jesus commend the Samaritan's faith because he expressed his faith in gratitude (Luke 14:15–16).[48] Thomas thus redefines the identity of a faith community by making it more inclusive and by rooting faith in gratitude rather than by making it 'ethnic' and 'territorial.' Such an inclusive definition is relevant in the pluralistic context of India.

Luke locates Jesus' saving deeds within the messianic expectations of the Jewish community as exemplified in Jesus' healing of a blind beggar (Luke 18:35–43). The beggar understood Jesus as the 'son of David' (Luke 18:36–38). This is because the Jews expected the Messiah to come from the lineage of king David and to "be appointed as the king of God's people, on the throne of David."[49] The physically blind man followed Jesus after receiving "sight" from him. But the Jewish leaders did not follow Jesus though they had 'sight.' For Luke, 'seeing' and 'following' Jesus is the sign of 'sight.' That being the case, the Jewish leaders were 'blind.' Therefore, for Thomas, faith means 'sight' or vision. Such a hermeneutical position is extremely vital in the pluralistic context of India.

Thomas' Hermeneutical Strategy: Summary Reflections

It is time to take stock of what we have observed in the above survey of Thomas' hermeneutical approach/es towards Jesus' miracles as chronicled in Luke's Gospel. Our inferences can be abridged fairly briefly.

a) Thomas unstintingly and solicitously embraces different approaches, ideologies and strategies in his spiritual journey which explains why he names his autobiography—*Ente Christava Dharmanveshana Paryadanam* [My Journey in Search of Christian Dharma].[50] He went through different stages in his hermeneutical journey before he arrived at the theological approach as known in his later books,

[47] Thomas, *In Jesus the Kingdom of God is Near*, 116.

[48] Thomas, *In Jesus the Kingdom of God is Near*, 116.

[49] Thomas, *In Jesus the Kingdom of God is Near*, 125.

[50] M. M. Thomas, *Ente Christava Dharmanveshana Paryadanam* (Tiruvalla: CSS, 2015 [1983]).

such as *Salvation and Humanisation.*[51] This is evident in his many hermeneutical approaches and strategies in his interpretation of Jesus' miracles in Luke. However, some of his contextual strategies do stand out in his commentaries, especially the one on Luke's Gospel.

b) Salvation as humanization is perhaps Thomas' most extensively used hermeneutical strategy in his commentary on Luke's Gospel. For Thomas, human person is God's gift.[52] But sin and satan dehumanize, disfigure and disintegrate humanity. Thomas uses the word 'demonic' to describe the power of sin over the collective life of the world. As a result of the disintegration of personality, humanity is unable to realise "personal destiny in relation to God, others and nature."[53] It is to such people that God offers a new humanity in Jesus which he makes possible through forgiveness of sins, exorcism and healing. Thomas interprets Jesus' miracles and the new humanism that they offer in the context of the struggle for human dignity in India and elsewhere.

c) 'Christocentric secularism' is another important contribution of Thomas. He interprets Jesus' healing of the leprosy affected person in the context of casteism in India and the untouchability associated with it. Thomas vehemently criticizes the dehumanizing religious and cultic laws that treat certain groups of people such as the dalits in India as 'polluted bodies.' Thomas even suggests that the word 'heal' may be used instead of 'clean' as the

---

[51] M. M. Thomas, *Salvation and Humanization: Some Critical Issues of the Theology of Mission in Contemporary India* (Madras: CLS, 1971). See also, Hielke T. Wolters, *Theology of Prophetic Participation: M. M. Thomas's Concept of Salvation and the Collective Struggle for Fuller Humanity in India* (Delhi/Bangalore: ISPCK/UTC, 1996), 12–74.

[52] Hielke T. Wolters, "Dr. M. M. Thomas' Theology of Prophetic Participation in Salvation and the Struggle for Humanisation" (Paper presented at the Seminar of the Birth Centenary of M. M. Thomas at Tiruvalla, 31 August 2015), 5.

[53] T. Jacob Thomas, *Ethics of a World Community: Contributions of Dr. M. M. Thomas based on Indian Reality* (Calcutta: Punthi Pustak, 1993), 152.

latter connotes 'impurity.' By his rehumanizing touch, Jesus declares that leprosy is only a physical disease and it does not necessarily make a person 'ritually unclean'. Thus Thomas calls for christocentric secularism, not 'closed secularism' but 'open secularism,'[54] where sick people need 'healing' not 'ritual cleansing,' and people are treated not on the basis of rituals and cultic laws but respected with dignity on the basis of the new humanity manifested in Jesus. Thomas argues, "Jesus Christ and the New Humanity offered in Him are … the spiritual foundation, the source of judgement, renewal and ultimate fulfilment of the struggle of mankind today for its humanity."[55] For Thomas, new humanity is a secular humanity which transcends 'cultic' boundaries.[56]

d) Thomas also employs 'christocentric inclusivism' as his method to interpret Jesus' miracles in Luke's Gospel. While interpreting Jesus' attitude towards the gentiles, Thomas contends, Luke has Jesus crossing the ethnic boundaries to rehumanize the dehumanized. Jesus appreciates the faith of the gentiles and heals them and thus challenges the ritual and cultic legitimacy of ethnic boundaries. For Thomas, the new humanity in Jesus offers salvation and divine forgiveness to all and thus human beings experience fulfillment of their personhood, creativity and increased freedom, and is redeemed in such a way that they are enabled to make their contribution to the salvation of the world. Such an inclusive community, rooted in the new humanity in Jesus, is an ekklēsial *koinonia* of forgiveness.

e) In his interpretation of miracles, Thomas assumes that salvation is holistic. This is very evident in his elucidation of Jesus' feeding of the multitude. Luke positions the

---

[54] Thomas, *The Church's Mission and Post-Modernism*, 12–13, 25; T. Jacob Thomas (Ed.), *M. M. Thomas Reader: Selected Texts on Theology, Religion and Society* (Tiruvalla: CSS, 2002), 164–166.

[55] Thomas, *Salvation and Humanization*, 4.

[56] Thomas, *The Church's Mission and Post-Modernism,* 42–43.

feeding miracle not only as the fulfillment of the messianic expectation but also as continuation of the holistic salvation God offered his people in Moses. The God of Israel who politically liberated his people from Egypt is the one who met their physical needs for food and water in the wilderness. Thomas does not see any tension between spiritual, political and physical dimensions of salvation.

f) Missiology is another tool that Thomas uses in his commentary. For Thomas, Jesus' command to his disciples to feed the hungry is not a one-off statement. Instead, it is a command to the church to minister to the thousands of people in India who suffer extreme poverty. Furthermore, according to Thomas, Jesus' healing miracles in no way undermine the importance of the church's hospital ministry because Jesus can heal people with and without physicians. Thomas also highlights the need for cooperating with the public medical services of the state and thus ensuring equitable health service to all the citizens. More importantly, Thomas envisions church as a healing/therapeutic community.

g) Thomas approaches Jesus' miracles in Luke from the vantage point of christology too. He argues that Jesus' miracles testify his divine authority as the son of God over all the satanic forces, sin and death, and signals the arrival of the kingdom of God, salvation and new humanism.

h) According to Thomas, Luke uses the traditions of Jesus' miracles from an ekklēsiological perspective. Jewish leaders would have severely criticised the Lukan community for their preaching of forgiveness of sins, healings and welcoming of the gentiles. By incorporating Jesus' miracles—forgiving the sins of the paralytic, healing of the leprosy affected person by touching him, raising of the dead—and his attitude towards the gentiles, Luke validates not only the kerygma of his community but also the very existence of his community itself.

To sum up, what is Thomas' hermeneutical strategy? There is no one single, uniform approach or strategy that he adopts to interpret Jesus' miracles recorded in Luke. Thomas' reading strategy is not eclectic either. Rather his hermeneutics is 'inspired hermeneutics.' In his spiritual journey, he has been influenced and inspired by various ideologies and political praxis, ranging from evangelical and sacramental piety to Marxism and liberation theology. But he was very critical of all these influences throughout his theological journey. Thomas never fully embraced Marxism and rejected its totalitarian interpretations of human reality. He also criticized liberation theology for its materialistic understanding of salvation. For Thomas, liberation which God offers in Jesus is not just liberation from social injustice and oppression, but also from sin and death. Human person as the divine gift appears to be the ground for Jesus' saving miracles because the liberative goal of the miracles is to initiate a 'cruciform humanity' which is a secular humanity free from dehumanizing social, political and ekklēsial forces. Thomas invites us to reimagine Jesus' miracles as a perpetual epiphanic possibility to rehumanize the dehumanized humanity and thus to continue to reveal the glory of humanity manifested in Jesus on the 'mount of transfiguration', and not to deem it as a 'closed epiphany.'

Chapter 4

Paul's Self-Description as 'Aborted Apostle' (1 Corinthians 15:8) A Foucauldian Reading

Introduction

Paul's self-positioning as an 'aborted apostle'[1] (ἐκτρώμα) is not a broadly discussed theme in the entire Pauline corpus. Paul reconstructs his apostolic identity and subjectivity by using an 'abnormal' choice of words. Why does Paul employ such 'derogatory' categories to define his identity? Does it mean that Paul succumbed to the dominant discourses on apostolicity? Was it a conscious attempt to interrogate the institutions of apostolicity and thereby re-constituting his subjectivity? This essay attempts to engage Paul's discourse on his

[1] The word ἐκτρώμα means "untimely born, abnormal, miscarriage, aborted etc." In this essay, the word "aborted" means the various attempts of the Jerusalem apostles to destroy Paul's apostolic existence, credentials, and identity. Since this essay concentrates on the subjectivity of Paul and power struggles that constitute it, I would use this translation more frequently. But certainly, other meanings are not undermined.

apostolicity by using Michel Foucault's understanding of subjectivity. It is assumed that Paul's self-description ('aborted apostle') refers to his 'enforced position' in the apostolic institution. The underlying tension is between the Jerusalem/Palestinian and diaspora apostles.[2] However, the discussion of Paul's resistance to dominant discourses on apostolicity is confined to 1 Corinthians.

Foucauldian Understanding of Subjectivity

a) Discourse and Knowledge/Truth

According to Foucault, discourse[3] means the "practices that systematically form the objects of which they speak."[4] It is entrenched in human practices and institutions within which the language is used in particular way. In other words, discourses are "ways of constituting knowledge, together with social practices, forms subjectivity and power relations, which inhere in such knowledges and relations between them."[5] Discourses produce and are not something that

---

[2] The Jerusalem/Palestinian apostolic band consists of 12 apostles who had the honour of associating with earthly/historical Jesus. Since Jerusalem was the locus of Jesus' life and mission, the twelve considered themselves as having superiority over the other disciples especially those from the diaspora. Consequently, Peter, James and John were called "super apostles." The Jerusalem lobby taught that only the Jerusalem apostles who had the vision of resurrection, are authentic and the remaining apostles are "lesser apostles." They used this discursive framework (see next foot note fir its meaning) in the discourse of apostolicity to exclude others like Paul. So, it was impossible for them to include Paul in the genuine apostolic band.

[3] For Foucault, a discourse is a strongly bounded area of social knowledge, a system of statements within which the world can be known. It is through discourse itself that the world is brought into being. Those who engage come to an understanding about themselves, their relationship to each other and their place in the world. Discourse is the complex of signs and practices that organized social existence and social reproduction. Each discourse has certain set of organizing rules/norms called discursive framework which demarcate the boundaries of discourses. See Sara Mills, *Discourse* (London and New York: Routledge, 1997), 17-18.

[4] Michel Foucault, *The Archaeology of Knowledge* (Translated by Sheridan Smith A. M., 1969, reprint; London: Tavistock Publishers, 1972), 49.

[5] Geoff Danaher et al., *Understanding Foucault* (Delhi: Motilal Banarsidas Publishers, 2001), 31.

exist in and of itself. Consequently, we can say that every discourse is historically inflected and political.

Discourses are everywhere. They are the 'stuff of society' and mediate all aspects of life.[6] Nevertheless, Foucault is concerned with the mechanics by which one discourse becomes dominant. Foucault argues that power operates in the processing of information concerning a 'fact.'[7] This process of production of knowledge took place by excluding other. Those in positions of authority subject it to a thorough method of ratification and thus produce truth.[8]

To be more precise, there is no objective truth since truth is produced by power. Truth is about some knowledge and practiced in social relationships. Those who have power have control of what is known and the way it is known, and who have such knowledge have power over those who do not. That is, "truth is not outside of power or lacking in power."[9] It means that truth is not innate to discourse rather it is constructed or 'manufactured.' Hence, Foucault opines that each society has its own "regimes of truth." Thus, truth, power and knowledge are intricately interrelated and what we need to examine is the mechanism of power in the construction of knowledge.

b) Power/Knowledge

For Foucault, knowledge is not objective but rooted in power relations. There is no power relation without the correlative constitution

---

[6] S. L. Joshi, *Modernity, Postmodernity and Neo-Sociological Theories* (New Delhi: Rawat Publications,2003), 281.

[7] Colin Gordon, ed., *Power/Knowledge. Selected Interviews and Other Writings 1972-1977 Michel Foucault* (Translated by Colin Gordon, et al., New York: Pantheon Books, 1980), 133.

[8] Michel Foucault, *Discipline and Punish. The Birth of the Prison* (Middlesex: Penguin Books, 1982), 26-29; Avijith Pathak, *Modernity, Globalization and Identity. Towards a Reflexive Quest* (New Delhi: Aakar Books, 2006), 36-37.

[9] For Foucault, truth is a system of ordered procedures for the production, regulation, distribution, circulation and operation of statements. See Michel Foucault, "Truth and Power", in *Orientalism. A Reader*, edited by Alexander Lyon Macfie (Washington Square, New York: New York University Press, 2000), 42.

of a field of knowledge or episteme.[10] Dominant practices declare knowledge as true. Truth/knowledge is not detached from structures or institutions that exercize power. Therefore, assertions of truth are assertions of power.[11] More exactly, all knowledges are claims and routes to power as well. The compound 'power/knowledge' describes that the relationship between power and knowledge is not oppositional but, rather, mutually constitutive. Relations of power and knowledge are not fixed forms of distribution; they are "matrices of transformation."

c) Concept of Power

Foucault understands power as the "multiplicity of force relations." In his significant writing, *The History of Sexuality*, Foucault clearly explains power as follows:[12]

1) Power comes from everywhere because discourses are everywhere.
2) Power is not located in certain centres or identifiable agencies or institutions.

---

[10] Episteme is the theory of knowledge that gives order to everyday life and mode of thought supplied with culture. It is the precondition of thought. No episteme is final. Therefore, there are epistemes. We need to deconstruct our epistemologies.

[11] Foucault, therefore, uses power /knowledge interchangeably. Spivak argues that the French word *pouvoir/ savoir* can be translated as power/ knowledge. Spivak warns us that if it is seen as the only translation, it monumentalizes Foucault unnecessarily. *Pouvoir* is of course "power." But there is also a sense of "can-do"-ness in "*pouvoir.*" See Gayatri Chakravorty Spivak, "More on Power/ knowledge," in The *Spivak Reader. Selected Works of Gayatri Chakravorty Spivak*, edited by Donna Landry and Gerald MacLean (London and New York: Routledge, 1996), 150-151; Mark K. George, "Foucault," in *Handbook of Postmodern Biblical Interpretation*, edited by A. K. M. Adams.1989, first published (St.Louis, Missouri: Chalice Press, 2000), 94-95.

[12] Michel Foucault, *The History of Sexuality. An Introduction*, vol. 1, translated by Robert Hurley, 1976, reprinted (London: Penguin Books, 1990), 92-95. See also Joseph Rouse, "Power/Knowledge", in *The Cambridge Companion to Foucault*, edited by Gary Gutting, 1994, reprinted (Cambridge: Cambridge University Press, 1996), 103-104.

3) It is diffused/disseminated/circulated or exercized in social relations.
4) Relations of power are not in a position of exteriority with respect to other types of relationships (economic processes, knowledge relationships, sexual relations).
5) Power comes from below.
6) Power relations are both intentional and nonsubjective as there is no power that is exercized without a series of aims and objectives.
7) Thus, it is apparent that power circulates. It has a 'capillary form of existence.' It produces things, induces knowledge, and produces discourse. Therefore, for Foucault, power is productive, polymorphous and subjectless in nature.

d) Power and Resistance

All power relationships imply a strategy of struggle. Consequently, Foucault argues that "where there is power, there is resistance…this resistance is never in a position of exteriority in relation to power."[13] It means that resistance does not exist outside of the power relations. It is, instead, intrinsically part of the relation because power is not a scheme of domination with an 'inside' or an 'outside.' Resistance is circulated in an uneven manner in relations of power. In other words, we can say that power is co-constituted by those who sustain and resist it. Therefore, social change is constantly realizable.[14]

e) Discourse, Power, and Subjectivity

It is through discourses that the objects about which they speak come into being. Discourses are embedded in human practices and institutions. It sets the limits and possibilities of existence. With in it, there are norms about the language of the discourse which is dictated by those in positions of authority. If one vocabulary is deficient, the

[13] Foucault, *The History of Sexuality*, 95.

[14] Critics say that Foucault has not properly developed the notion of "genealogy of resistance." They say that though Foucault talks about micro level resistance, he does not discuss the modalities of local struggles. See S. Panneerselvam, "A Critique of Foucault's Power and Knowledge," *IPQ* xxvii/ 1&2 (January-April 2000), 27.

people coin new vocabulary. Hence, the language of the discourse is primary, because the content of the discourse is being shaped by its language. In other words, language of the discourse shapes the objects of the discourse.

Such discourses position us in the conversation.[15] It determines the position of the person which should be occupied in the conversation. Eventually, it imposes a social order or ordering and reinforces the enforced 'fixity' of identity. It is also a conditioning. Through this positioning, the understanding of self is formed as desired by those in positions of authority.

Power dispersed in the social relations form 'practices'. In addition, practices give us a disciplining of the self. Foucault says that power/knowledge produce in individuals a sense of their own subjectivity and an awareness of their status as 'subjects.' Subjects are simultaneously created and controlled by the knowledge produced about individuals. Discourses determine the position of the person and through positioning our subjectivity is produced. Therefore, it is clear that power shapes and constitutes subjectivity rather than simply repressing it. In other words, subjectivity is shaped and constituted by power: it is essentially its construct.

Competing Discourses of Apostolicity

Gerd Theissen convincingly analyzes the tension between the Jerusalem apostles and Paul.[16] They belong to two different groups: itinerant charismatics and community organizers.[17] They arose in Palestinian region and Hellenistic region respectively. As protagonists

---

[15] It means the discourse in action.

[16] I admit with the fact that Gerd Theissen is basically a profound sociological interpreter of the New Testament and not an ardent Foucauldian. But his analysis is used here because it provides us some pertaining ideas with regard to the intense rift between the Jerusalem band and Paul based on the functional style of the apostle. Here 'style' can be correlated with the episteme and discursive framework of the discourse of apostolicity. The Jerusalem apostles used this episteme to sideline others like Paul who belonged to diaspora.

[17] Gerd Theissen, *The Social Setting of Pauline Christianity. Essays on Corinth*, translated by John H. Schutz, 1982, second fortress press paperback printing (Philadelphia: Fortress Press, 1989), 28-40.

of Hellenistic mission, Paul, unlike the itinerant charismatics or wandering missionaries, renounced their privilege of material support and hospitality. As opposed to customary and normally accepted norm of legitimacy Paul put across three 'odd' norms: charismatic legitimation, traditional legitimation, and functional legitimation.[18]

The entire issue of authentic apostolicity started with Paul's claim to be of the rank of Jerusalem apostle (1 Cor 9:1-2; 3-11). The Jerusalem band of apostles decided the credibility of apostolicity. They simply dictated even the discursive framework of apostolicity. They had no difficulty in accommodating Paul as 'missionary apostle.'[19] The apostle's defensive remarks in 9:1–2 and 15:8–9 presuppose criticisms against his apostolic credentials. Paul's self-commendation as the model to imitate (4:16; 11:1) may have intensified the opposition to him.

The episteme of the discourse on apostolicity by the Jerusalem group has got three discursive features:[20]

1. Authentic apostle should have had the fortune of associating with Jesus.
2. Apostle should have the vision of the risen Christ (1 Cor 9:2a).
3. Genuine apostles have to accept means of sustenance from the flock.

The predominant discourse on apostolicity was exercized by the Jerusalem band. They had the power to 'validate' and verify apostolicity. Their understanding/knowledge about the nature and function of an apostle was considered true. Paul did not witness resurrection. Therefore, Paul's calling to apostolic office could not

---

[18] Gerd Theissen, *The Social Setting of Pauline Christianity*, 42-54.

[19] Hans Dieter Betz, "Corinthians, First Letter of," in *The Anchor Bible Dictionary*, vol. 1, edited by David Noel Freedman (New York: Doubleday, 1992), 1141.

[20] Gerd Luedemann, *Opposition to Paul in Jewish Christianity*, translated by M.Eugene Boring, 1983, English language edition (Minneapolis: Fortress Press, 1989), 67-68. See also C. Brown, "ἐκτρώμα", in *The New International Dictionary of New Testament Theology*, edited by Colin Brown, vol. 1[A-F] (Exeter: The Paternoster Press, 1975), 183.

take place in the 'normal' and organic sequence. In other words, Paul 'essentially lacks'[21] the traits of an apostle.

Moreover, Paul's calling is forced and abnormal. It was an 'irregular'/'sudden' conversion[22] as far as the Jerusalem apostles are concerned. A difficult relationship existed between Paul and Jerusalem apostles after Antioch (Gal 2:11-14).[23] As a result, Paul, 'abnormal apostle,' was singled out as a 'heretic' by the 'proper apostle.' Paul's experience of the vision of the risen Christ was not taken as valid as per their norms. Any apostle who contradicts with their 'truth' discourse would be branded as the 'other' or 'unfit' or 'insane.' In short, the non-Jerusalem/diaspora apostle has been 'strategically essentialized,' stigmatized and 'fixed' Paul in zones of 'peripherality'.

Therefore, the Jerusalem apostolic band called Paul a 'miscarriage' (ἐκτρώμα). The word ἐκτρώμα suggests the characteristics of an "unformed, undeveloped, repulsive, and possibly lifeless foetus."[24] It is a term of insult or abuse. This process of 'othering' made Paul an 'aborted foetus.' The question is who has the power to 'normalize' or make a person an authentic apostle. It is in this context that Paul enters into the discourse of apostolicity and interrogates the very episteme and discursive framework of apostolicity.

---

[21] It assumes that groups, classes of objects have defining features exclusive to all members of that category. In other words, essential characteristics distinguishing one race from other. It is called strategic essentialism. It means that humanity is divided into unchanging natural types.

[22] James Moffat, *The First Epistle of Paul to the Corinthians*, 1938, 7th impression (London: Holder and Stoughton Limited, 1951), 238.

[23] The battle cry is circumcision versus foreskin. See Brigitte Kahl, "Reading Galatians and Empire at the Great Altar of Pergamon," *Union Seminary Quarterly Review* 59/3-4 (2005), 38.

[24] C. K. Barrett, *A Commentary on the First Epistle to the Corinthians*, Black Commentary Series, 1968, 2nd edition reprint (London: T&T Black, 1994), 344.

'Εκτρώμα as a Counter Discourse[25]

Paul did not subscribe to the imposed subjectivity. Rather Paul engages the very same discourse and interrogates it. 'Εκτρώμα was used by those who exercized the powerful discourse to 'objectify' or 'thingify' those who are not 'fit' in the institution of apostolicity. It literally means 'untimely birth,' 'miscarriage' or 'abortion.'[26] It is used thrice in LXX.[27] The decisive feature is the 'abnormal' time of birth and the 'unfinished' form of thus born. The main emphasis is on the 'abnormality' of the process, which took place when the Lord had ceased to manifest himself to the apostles. It also means the 'abnormality' of Paul's position in the chain of apostolicity.[28] Paul resists the discourse of the 'essentially sufficient' and initiates a counter discourse.

'Εκτρώμα must have been used by Paul's opponents as an offensive term to put him down. In order to reinforce 'fixity,' Paul's opponents used this contemptuous language to shape the object

---

[25] Richard Terdiman coined this term to characterize the theory and practice of resistance. The confrontation between the constructed reality and its subversion as the locus of change. Dominant discourses can absorb the would be resistances. The ways in which resistance to a dominant discourse might come from the margins. It raises the issue of subversion of the so called 'canonical' discourses and imposed conditioning.

[26] Schneider, "ἐκτρώμα," in *Theological Dictionary of the New Testament*, edited by Gerhard Kittel, translated by Geoffrey W. Bromiley, vol. 2 [D-H], 1964, reprint (Grand Rapids, Michigan: William B. Eerdmans Publishing Company, 1974): 465. For detailed discussion of the term and previous interpretation, please see Matthew W. Mitchell, "Re-examining the 'Aborted Apostle': An Exploration of Paul's self-Description in 1 Corinthians 15:8", in *Journal of the Study of the New Testament* 25/4 (June 2003): 470-476; Anthony C. Thistleton, *The First Epistle to the Corinthians. A Commentary on the Greek Text* (Grand Rapids, Michigan: William B. Eerdmans Publishing Company, 2000), 1208-1211.

Scholars like Muller attributes unworthiness to be called an apostle. See H. Muller, "ἐκτρώμα," in *The New International Dictionary of New Testament Theology*, edited by Colin Brown, vol 1[A-F] (Exeter: The Paternoster Press, 1975), 183. For Luedemann it is not abuse, rather a self-description: see Gerd Luedemann, *Opposition to Paul in Jewish Christianity*, 260.

[27] In Num 12:12; Job 3:16 and Ecc 6:3. See Schneider, "ἐκτρώμα:" 465.

[28] William F. Orr, and James Arthur, *1 Corinthians,* The Anchor Bible (New York: Doubleday, 1976), 318.

of their discourse. The Jerusalem crew tried to 'abort' his apostolic identity and existence. Because for them, Paul, a diaspora apostle, was an unwanted, undesired and mistaken apostle.

But, Paul took upon himself the forced and mocking attribute as a 'badge of honor.' He 'gate crashed' into the exclusive and hallowed number, the twelve. Paul questions the unquestionable and 'canonical' epistemes that 'abort' his very apostolic being and the ontological privilege of the Jerusalem apostles to verify his apostolic qualification. The ability to check the validity of the apostolicity will give them the power to condition subjectivity. He 'intrudes into' the marked spaces determined by the 'hallowed twelve' and deconstructs the language of the discourse of apostolicity.

Paul presents his apostolic credentials as a counter discourse. He positions himself in the apostolic lineage as a normal experience over against the unusual and strained positioning. The Pauline counter discourse has the following epistemological, subversive and theological nuances:

a) Ἐκτρῶμα as re-positioning: Paul uses ἐκτρῶμα to re-position himself who was by now and forcefully positioned by the Jerusalem apostles. Positioning has a vital role in the formation of subjectivity because it sets the restrictions and potentials of existence. Our subjectivity is formed in relation to the dominant discourse rampant in the society. Paul realized that discourse of apostolicity determines the position in the institution of apostolicity. Paul relentlessly criticizes the exclusive and repressive 'privilege' of the Jerusalem apostles to authenticate his apostolicity.

   In order to relocate his position, Paul rather subversively positions himself in the whole succession/chain of apostolicity. He uses the phrase 'ἔσχατον δὲ πάντων' ('last of all') as a critique of the Jerusalem discourse of apostolicity. Here the word ἔσχατον (meaning 'last') is not in the same sense as the Jerusalem lobby used. For them, Paul is rather an abnormal 'late comer.' He was not born at the right time for the ministry to which he was called.

Paul negates the Jerusalem 'chronological periodization' and suggests eternity as subversive logic. But, it must be noted that Paul's use of the word πάντων (meaning 'of all') is for the inclusive/collective nature of apostolicity. Paul does not negate the validity of Jerusalem apostles, but positions himself in the collective institution of apostolicity, irrespective of its geographical trope. Through this counter discourse Paul re-positions himself and negates all kinds of topographical, genetic and sequential superiority.

b) *Ἐκτρώμα as resisting strategic essentializing*: Paul belongs to the diaspora/non-Jerusalem regime of apostles. Consequently, for the Jerusalem apostles, Paul 'essentially lacks' the qualities to become a genuine/legitimate apostle. In addition, Paul did not serve a period of apprenticeship and discipleship with the earthly/historical Jesus and did not adhere to the itinerant and the so-called 'normal' mode of apostolicity. Besides, Paul could not witness the risen Lord along with the Jerusalem apostles. Damascus appearance was by all reason far removed from its expected time frame. The net result was that he was not as acceptable as the twelve apostles. His commission was not an ordinary, organic process like theirs.

   Hence, the Palestinian apostles branded him as a 'lesser apostle.' By adopting the same discursive framework of the discourse of apostolicity, Paul negated the predatory conception of essentialism. Essentialism falsely represents Paul as 'ontologically inferior.' It was an attempt to reconstitute his subjectivity and decriminalize all kinds of 'othering.' It can produce in persons a kind of subjectivity and a sense of their own position as subjects.

c) Ἐκτρώμα *as celebrating "capillary apostolicity:"* During the life time of Paul, apostolicity was considered as something 'out there' at Jerusalem. The discourse on apostolicity literally 'fixed' and 'closed' the institution of apostolicity. But, for Paul, the institution of apostolicity extends itself in 'capillary fashion.'[29] It means that the endowment of apostolicity cannot be fixed in a specific place or person. Any effort to do otherwise would invite diverse resistance in the form of counter discourse.

It is interesting to note that Paul's use of the term κἀμοί (καί+ἐγώ)[30] is an attempt to extend the so far fixed institution of apostolicity. The dispersed and circulated nature of apostolicity is brought to light over against the normal notion of identifiable and concealed centres of apostolicity. Any discourse that facilitates the notion that the 'apostolate' is exhausted by the completion of the normative witness, written and passed on to us as authoritative. That is to make of their commission and their communication a static, historical 'there-ness'. Apostolicity is not something that 'happened and ended' or a possession rather an open and inclusive invitation. It provides Paul a position in the hitherto negated institution of apostolicity and there by a new self-understanding.

d) Ἐκτρώμα *as reliving resurrection*:[31] In this subversive/ counter discourse, Paul opposes the Jerusalem discourse which 'fixes' resurrection as a past event.[32] It is not possible to contemporize the reality of resurrection. Therefore, resurrection appearances are the unique and exclusive genealogical privilege of the Jerusalem apostles. The Greek

---

[29] Apostolicity is not something that is acquired or seized. It is not located in certain centers or identifiable agencies or institutions nor is it a 'fixed.' It is diffused /disseminated/circulated or exercized. It has a 'capillary form of existence.' It means that apostolicity is dispersed in faith community as a whole irrespective of the chronological and geographical conditions. It is very much related to the 'diffused' nature of power.

[30] It means "also to me.'

[31] I agree with Gerd Luedemann that this text does not talk about resurrection rather apostolicity. See Gerd Luedemann, *Opposition to Paul in Jewish Christianity,* 70.

[32] Hanz Conzelmann, *1 Corinthians*, translated by James W. Leitch, 1969, English translation (Philadelphia: Fortress Press, 1975), 258.

word ὤφθη[33] means that the reality of resurrection was made available to Paul by the 'marvellously sufficient,' liberative and 'justifying grace of God.'[34] Paul uses ὤφθη—the aorist indicative passive tense of the word ὁράω—to de-privilege the vision of the reality of resurrection. The experience and knowledge of the reality of resurrection re-positions Paul in the discourse of resurrection and validates his apostolicity. It resists every endeavor to 'abort' his apostolic existence from being born.

e) Ἐκτρώμα *as counter discourse of 'third race*:'[35] Attitude towards gentiles was a major point of tension between Jerusalem apostles and Paul. The Jerusalem band of apostles confined the economy of salvation and institution of apostolicity to the house of Israel. So, they had no difficulty in excluding a diaspora apostle like Paul and the gentiles, unless circumcized. Paul rejected the 'absorptive capacity'[36] of the dominant discourse which 'naturalizes' the superiority of the Jerusalem band of apostles. But Paul, on the other hand, did not yield to such discourses. Instead, Paul subverted the 'canonical' horizons of apostolicity and repositioned his diasporic and apostolic identity.

Paul initiated the counter discourse as a movement that surpasses the parochial and trivial tension between diaspora and authentic apostolicity. He aimed toward a 'new creation' which would transcend all kinds of stigmatization and repressive binaries.

---

[33] It means "appeared."

[34] Johan Christiaan Beker, *Paul the Apostle. The Apocalyptic Triumph of God* (Philadelphia: Fortress Press, 1984), 7.

[35] It must be noted here that in this section the methodology of Sanders is not used. Instead, only the phrase "third race" is adopted. E.P.Sanders, *Paul, the Law, and the Jewish People*, 1983, first paperback printing (Minneapolis: Fortress Press, 1985), 173.

[36] The capacity of the dominant discourse to absorb/ignore/marginalize other discourses.

It is neither an ethnic identity[37] nor an exclusive fellowship of the 'aborted', rather an inclusive space. This 'new creation' is the 'church of God' or the 'third race.'

Conclusion

Paul's usage of the term 'aborted apostle' is a diasporic counter discourse which disrupts the dominant Palestinian discourse of apostolicity. It tries to retrieve the hitherto marginalized voices of the so called 'aborted' community of disciples. It also focuses on the way in which the diaspora 'abnormal' apostle, Paul, made use of, and went further than those strategies for survival and self-representation. Paul strategically interrogates the 'racialization' and 'essentialization' of apostolicity and exposed the capillary as well as the happening nature of apostolicity. Paul re-positioned himself in the apostolic institution by reliving the 'marvellously sufficient grace' of God unveiled through Damascus theophany. This re-positioning is the means of reconstructing Paul's apostolic self. To sum up, Pauline counter discourse, ἐκτρώμα, is a tactic, a practice and a process.

[37] It can be very well connected to postcolonial theory of "third space of enunciation."

Chapter 5

The Melchizedek Tradition and Jesus' High Priesthood

A Postcolonial Re-imagination of Christology in the Letter to the Hebrews

Introduction

For modern readers, it remains true that, in some ways, the book of Hebrews appears not only 'alien' and 'incomprehensible', but also "antiquated, irrelevant, and even esoteric:" and some scholars refer to Hebrews as syncretistic and 'contextualized religion' as it 'incorporates' many first-century religious and philosophical traditions and thought-forms which might have been called 'heathen' or pagan under certain circumstances. This may be because, traditionally, scholars incline to limit their discussions pertaining to the author's extensive use of various Jewish theological traditions, particularly the use of Melchizedek tradition, quotations and exegesis from the Hebrew Bible, to christological motifs. Furthermore, the theology of the sacrifice of Christ in Hebrews seems to be locked in the presuppositions of the past. This perhaps best explains the 'marginal' status of the epistle both in the canonical and in the broader context of the (re)search for 'subversive hermeneutics'—which overturn and dismantle totalizing perspectives that claim to be objective (neutral meaning), final, exhaustive, and prescriptive (definite meaning)—from which it was almost excluded. Such "marginality" would in itself call for a postcolonial investigation.

But, being a (somewhat) diaspora text, Hebrews has more to offer to the new liberative quest and zest for alternative hermeneutics that would not only (re)move, (re)position, and (re)define the 'margins', but also engage and interrogate the so-called 'margins' themselves, especially in the context of our renewed understanding of the liminality of human existence in the globalizing village. This paper, therefore, investigates the use of Melchizedek tradition in the Letter to the Hebrews from the vantage point of postcolonial biblical interpretation. The merit of a postcolonial reading of Hebrews includes its ability to find liberating strands in the texts, while showing up the text's or its reception history's complicity in imperialist endeavors.

(Re)Mapping the Audience of Hebrews

According to Nicholas Lash, "all human utterances occur in a context. And the contexts in which they occur modify their meaning."[1] Restating Lash, interpretation or hermeneutical activity does not take place in the abstract and is never neutral. Interpretation, therefore, is always done perspectivally—whether consciously or unconsciously. It implies, therefore, that biblical interpretation must take into account the influence and identification of the hermeneutical location.

This does fittingly account for a detailed investigation of the politics of the centripetal force of the interpretation of Hebrews: the historical and theological situatedness of the audience of the Hebrews. Instead of focusing on "the politics of identity," where very often identity is understood as essence,[2] this paper focuses on

[1] Nicholas Lash, *Theology on the Way to Emmaus* (London: SCM, 1986), 33.

[2] Mary Ann Tolbert, "Afterwords: Christianity, Imperialism, and the Decentering of Privilege," in *Reading from this Place:* Vol.1, *Social Location and*

"the politics of location" because, as Allison Jasper correctly observes, everyone belongs to and participates in a socio-political location and a member of a "distinct and identifiable social configuration," irrespective of the hybridity and heterogeneity of the human subjectivity.[3] In Tolbert's view, the subversively close connection between "the politics of identity" and "the politics of location," while challenging the essentialization of human subjectivity, calls for a sliding, "fluid, shifting, and generally context-dependent" identity.[4] And the constructed, evolving and emerging nature of human subjectivity depends, to a great extent, in the words of Jeremy Punt, on "'facts of blood' (social, personal and familial alignments) and 'facts of bread' (national, economic and political matters)."[5]

But, one cannot understand Hebrews without identifying the social and ethnic composition of its recipients. Firm evidence for the time at which Hebrews was written is almost entirely lacking; a judgment on this question depends on a 'balance of probabilities' which cannot be assessed with anything approaching certainty. Yet the balance of probabilities leads to prefer a date before the fall of Jerusalem. It is difficult to be more precise. The discussion must remain inconclusive due to the lack of internal evidence. While neither the case for nor the objections to a pre-70 C.E. date are conclusive and decisive, this paper assumes that Hebrews reads more naturally in a pre-70 C.E. setting.

The next assumption concerns the ethnic identity of the audience, which, this paper assumes, is very likely a mixed community of Jewish Christians and Gentile Christians,[6] but, as Paul

---

Biblical Interpretation in the United States (eds., Fernando F. Segovia and Mary Ann Tolbert; Minneapolis: Fortress, 1995), 305–16.

[3] Allison Jasper, "Communicating the Word of God," *JSNT*, 67:29–44.

[4] Tolbert, "Afterwords," 305–16.

[5] They are often at (violent) odds with one another. See Jeremy H. Punt, "The Letter to the Hebrews," in *A Postcolonial Commentary on the New Testament Writings* (eds. Fernando F. Segovia and R. S. Sugirtharajah; T&T Clark: London, 2009), 338-368, here 342.

[6] David A. DeSilva, *Perseverance in Gratitude: A Socio-Rhetorical Commentary on the Epistle "to the Hebrews"* (Grand Rapids, Michigan: Eerdmans, 2000), 2–3, 6–7.

Ellingworth rightly contends, predominantly Jewish Christians.[7] Some scholars have argued that the recipients of Hebrews must have been unconverted Essenes[8] or converted Essenes.[9] The exponents of this thesis have grounded their argument mainly on the use of Melchizedek by the two communities. But, the resemblances between the two communities are only superficial, not substantial; 11Q Melchizedek appears to represent Melchizedek as a supernatural figure, with function similar to that of angel Michael. Although both communities vehemently criticize Levitical priesthood and the Jerusalem cultus, the alternative for Qumran is that of a closed community governed by stricter religious and social rules, while the alternative for Hebrews is a community inclusive of non-Jews. Likewise, Qumran criticizes Jerusalem priesthood, Hebrews seeks to expose inadequacy of Levitical priesthood.

One can however easily make out the presence of Jewish Christians from the extensive use of the Old Testament, cultic regulations (Heb 9:1–10), tabernacle motif, and the Jewish exegetical rules which characterize rabbinic Judaism in the epistle.[10] Hebrews envisions one people of God; no break in salvation history;[11] Jews are not marginalized or demeaned.[12] It is necessary to address the question of supersessionism in Hebrews because it is closely related to the Jewish background of the recipients; there is no issue of if Christ 'supersedes' Judaism or church 'supersedes' Israel.[13] What we find in Hebrews is not Jewish messianic covenantalism, or attack

---

[7] Paul Ellingworth, *The Epistle to the Hebrews* (NIGTC; Grand Rapids, Michigan: Eerdmans, 1993), 27.

[8] H. Kosmala, *Hebräer, Essener, Christen* (Leiden: Brill, 1959).

[9] For detailed discussion see, F. F. Bruce, "'To the Hebrews? or To the Essenes'?," *NTS* 9 (1962–63): 217–32; Y. Yadin, "A Note on Melchizedek and Qumran," *IEJ* 15 (1965), 152–154.

[10] Gareth Lee Cockerill, *The Epistle to the Hebrews* (Grand Rapids, Michigan/ Cambridge, U.K.: Eerdmans, 2012), 19–23.

[11] Cockerill, *The Epistle to the Hebrews*, 21.

[12] Cockerill, *The Epistle to the Hebrews*, 23.

[13] Cockerill, *The Epistle to the Hebrews*, 22. See also Ben Witherington III, *Letters and Homilies for Jewish Christians*: A Socio-Rhetorical Commentary on Hebrews, James and Jude (Downers Grove, Illinois: IVP, 2007), 25.

on Judaism or its leaders.[14] Hays argues that Hebrews does not suggest that Jewish people have been replaced by gentile, instead new covenant as sustaining but transforming Israel's categories in the light of Christ event.[15] The title "to the Hebrews" (*Πρὸς Ἑβραίους*) however cannot be taken as conclusive evidence to establish the identity of the audience because the label is not traditional, rather than original.[16]

But, it does not require the recipients to be Jewish because Gentile Christians would also be familiar with the Old Testament (literary knowledge, not first-hand acquaintance with the procedure in the Jerusalem temple) and manifested a lively interest in the Mosaic tabernacle and Levitical offerings.[17] Hebrews 11 denationalizes the heroes of the Jewish heritage in order to make them heritage of Gentile Christians: "Hebrews…opened the way for Gentile Christians to read Israelite history as if it were their own."[18] The mentioning of Timothy (13:23) strongly suggests that the audience must have formed as part of Paul's mission, which had its explicit goal of ministering to the gentiles.[19]

---

[14] Richard B. Hays, "'Here We have No lasting city:' New Covenantalism in Hebrews," in *The Epistle to the Hebrews and Christian Theology* (eds., Richard Bauckham et. al; Grand Rapids, Michigan/Cambridge, U.K.: Eerdmans, 2009), 151–173.

[15] Hays, "Here We have No lasting city," 151–73.

[16] Donald Hagner, *Hebrews* (Grand Rapids, Michigan: BakerBooks, 1983), 2. But Witherington is of the view that "to the Jews" should not be considered as a mere conjecture; for him, "to the Jews" means "to the Jewish Christians." See *Letters and Homilies for Jewish Christians*, 24.

[17] Jason A. Whitlark, *Resisting Empire: Rethinking the Purpose of the Letter to "the Hebrews"* (LNTS 484; London: Bloomsbury T&T Clark, 2014), 14–15; Richard B. Hays, *The Conversion of the Imagination: Paul as Interpreter of Israel's Scripture* (Grand Rapids: Eerdmans, 2006), viii; DeSilva, *Perseverance in Gratitude*, 6–7.

[18] Pamela M. Eisenbaum, *The Jewish Heroes of Christian History: Hebrews 11 in Literary Context* (SBLDS 156; Atlanta: Scholars, 1997), 220; see 187–88, 218–25 for details.

[19] David A. DeSilva, *The Letter to the Hebrews in Social Scientific Perspective* (Eugene, Oregon: Cascade, 2012), 35.

In light of the above considerations, separately or even together, it is best to assume that the recipients of Hebrews were predominantly but not exclusively Jewish Christian. As Cockerill fittingly notes, Hebrews does not employ any ethnic categories to define its first readers;[20] 'Jewish Christians' are "followers of Christ who have been acculturated into and continue to be attracted by Jewish religious practices regardless of their ethnicity."[21] Such acculturation may have happened to the gentiles too primarily because many of their fellow believers were Jews. More importantly, gentiles identified themselves with the synagogues as God-fearers. On the one hand, the audience of Hebrews was loyal to Christ, and on the other hand very particular about having continuous association with Jewish practices.[22] This explains why there is no direct polemic in the first 12 chapters of the epistle rejecting Judaism,[23] rather a completionist argument;[24] there is no comparison or supersessionism of Christ contemporary Judaism but with the Old Testament institutions and Levitical priesthood. Therefore, the terms 'Jewish Christians' and 'Gentile Christians' may be used in a religious sense, not in an ethnic sense.[25] It shows the sensitivity of the author towards the ethnic texture of the audience. Had there been only either one of them, the epistle would not have displayed such exemplary and characteristic ethnic sensitivity.

The primary piece of external evidence points to the presence of Hebrews in Rome comes from *1 Clement.* 1 Clem 36:1–5 which calls Jesus 'high priest' (cf. 3:1) is taken from much of Heb 1:3–14.[26] The "shared terminology and contextual issues between

---

[20] Cockerill, *The Epistle to the Hebrews*, 20.

[21] Cockerill, *The Epistle to the Hebrews*, 20.

[22] Cockerill, *The Epistle to the Hebrews*, 20

[23] Cockerill, *The Epistle to the Hebrews*, 20–21; cf. the sustained *synkrisis* (comparison) with the Levitical cultus serves the ideological need of the Gentile readers, not the mixed community.

[24] Witherington III, *Letters and Homilies for Jewish Christians*, 26; Ellingworth, *Hebrews*, 24.

[25] Cockerill, *The Epistle to the Hebrews*, 20

[26] Cf. for DeSilva, the use of Hebrews in *1 Clement* is not a conclusive proof of the Roman destination, given the mobility first-century Christ followers. See *Perseverance in Gratitude*, 22.

Hebrews and other documents of Roman provenance" also connect Hebrews to Rome.[27] Timothy, mentioned in Heb 13:23, was also known to Roman church (cf. Rom 16:21).[28] Like the first recipients of Hebrews, Roman church also had suffered persecution (6:10–13; 10:32–34) and was known for generosity.[29] Eusebius reports the history of Rome's rejection of Pauline authorship of Paul (*Hist. eccl.* 3.3.4-5; 6.20.3).[30] Jerome also gives hint concerning the reservation of the 'Latins' to accept canonicity of Hebrews partly because of the uncertainty concerning its authorship (*Epist.* 129.3).[31] All these data have been considered collectively, making it more natural to see Rome as the original destination of Hebrews, which is the fundamental assumption for this study.

It is evident from the above discussions that the very nature and character of the followers of Christ as in Hebrews is diasporic. They are "flesh-and-believers struggling to overcome the stranglehold of past traditions and adjust to the fresh movements of God in their fast-changing world."[32] As a diaspora community in Rome, the first recipients of Hebrews would have definitely engaged the Roman imperial forces and its claims. Religiously and politically speaking, the audience of Hebrews were outside the 'margins' of the mainline Judaism and of the Roman imperial system; both Jewish leaders and the Roman powers 'marginalized' them. It created a 'displaced' situation where they had to live in 'many worlds' at the same time.

[27] The word Hebrews uses for "leaders" (ἡγουμένοις—Heb 13:7, 17, 24) was very frequently employed at Rome (*1 Clem* 1:3; 21:6; Herm. *Vis.* 2.2.6; 3.9.7) use the same terminology for leaders; the generosity described in Heb 6:10–11 echoes the characteristic generosity of the early christians in Rome (Lane, *Hebrews*, lviii); the issue of apostasy discussed in Heb 6:4–6; 12:16–17 recalls the issue concerning the possibility of repentance from apostasy or post-baptismal sin debated Christ followers in Rome (Her. *Vis.* 5.7; cf. *Sim.* 9.20.1–21.3). See for details, Whitlark, *Resisting Empire*, 7–8.

[28] Hagner, *Hebrews*, 5

[29] Hagner *Hebrews*, 5.

[30] Whitlark, *Resisting Empire*, 8.

[31] Whitlark, *Resisting Empire*, 8.

[32] Ray C. Stedman, *Hebrews* (IVPCS; Downers Grove, Illinois: IVP, 1992), 9; Alan M. Stibbs, *So Great Salvation: The Meaning and Message of the Letter to the Hebrews* (CSL; Exeter: Paternoster, 1970), 9–12.

On the one hand, they lived in Roman and Jewish world, and on the other hand, they could not live in any of these worlds. They did not belong anywhere because both the Jews and the Romans viewed them as 'undesirables' and 'misfit'; they could not call either the Jewish world or the Roman political world their home. The reality of such a way of life creates a situation where diasporic people exist as "permanent strangers" in the Roman world and as "permanent aliens" in the Jewish world.[33]

Both the Jewish leaders and the Roman imperialist powers 'pushed' the readers of Hebrews to the so-called 'margins' through ideological and political discourses. This 'epistemic behavior' achieves its effectivity through the practice of exclusion. Consequently, the dominant discourses of the Romans and the Jews 'fix' the boundaries/margins of the first readers as a result of their loyalty to Christ (10:32–34; 11:1–40; 12:1–11).[34] The fixation of boundaries is sinful as it 'fixes' people in 'zones' of dependency and 'peripherally.' Ellingworth categorizes the dangers facing the recipients of the epistle as *passive* (lassitude, neglect, and immaturity), *active* (apostasy), and *external* (the pressure of ostracism and persecution).[35] The persecution included public harassment, imprisonment, confiscation of property, but had fallen short of martyrdom (12:4). 12:4 contains a growing hostility against the believers and impending martyrdom that they want to avoid.[36]

The anxiety at the oppressive and traumatic 'othering' and 'subjectification' may have been exacerbated by the delay of Christ's

---

[33] Fernando F. Segovia, "Toward a Hermeneutics of the Diaspora: A Hermeneutics of otherness and Engagement," in *Reading from This Place: Vol.1, Social Location and Biblical Interpretation in the United States* (eds., Fernando F. Segovia and M. A. Tolbert; Minneapolis: Fortress, 1995), 57–73, here 61–65.

[34] Punt, "The Letter to the Hebrews," 361.

[35] Ellingworth, *Hebrews*, 78–79. The present exposition assumes that there challenges were not separate but closely related.

[36] DeSilva, *Perseverance in Gratitude*, 17; Graham Hughes, *Hebrews and Hermeneutics: The Epistle to the Hebrews as a New Testament Example of Biblical Interpretation* (Cambridge: Cambridge University Press, 1979), 28; Witherington III, *Letters and Homilies for Jewish Christians*, 27, 28, 29–30, 32; Raymond Brown, *The Message of Hebrews* (Downers Grove, Illinois: IVP Academic, 1982), 13, 17.

return (1:14; 10:36–39), rejection of the gospel (2:1–4; 5:11–6:8; 10:26–31; 12:14–17), and apostasy from Christ (6:1–18; 10:26–31). Some people have not fully grasped the full significance of what Christ had done and the continuing efficacy of his saving activity (5:11–6:8; 12:13) and abstained from worship (10:24–25).[37] Apostasy was a live option for the audience (2:3; 3:12; 6:4–6; 10:29). Therefore, people would have decided to renounce christian faith and go back to Judaism.[38] It is natural to get attracted to privileges of the synagogues that would be theirs by compromising their faith and identifying with the imperial forces (12:14–17). They are like Esau who sold his birth right for a meal (12:16–17). Many, if not all, seems to have been frightened by the disparagement and marginalization that they suffered as result of their christian faith (11:1–41). They had "drifted away" from the message they had received (2:1–4).[39]

The author, however, exhorts his audience not to succumb to 'othering' and marginalization but to "resist evil" (12:4). As with any other diasporic community, "ethnocentric politics of identity" is one possibility and practice insular and separate existence. But ethnocentric practice, which might be inevitable, would not only seal off all the possibilities of crossing the borders/boundaries but also can lead (though unintentionally) to "xenophobic rhetorics," "ethnic self-aggrandizement" and destructive essentialism. Return to universalization could very likely result in the universalization of dominant cultures and associated hierarchical values. More importantly, any attempt to evade interethnic critiques and moving the margins, in the well-chosen phrase of Homi Bhabha, would invite the danger of being seduced by "celebratory romance of the past" or by an attempt at "homogenizing the history of the present."[40]

What then is the real alternative to "ethnocentric insularity" or "enclosed community?" Is it universalization? According to

---

[37] DeSilva, *The Letter to the Hebrews in Social Scientific Perspective*, 50.

[38] According DeSilva, it is "pedestrian inability" to live within the lower status, not persecution and attraction to Judaism that motivated apostasy. See *Perseverance in Gratitude*, 19.

[39] Cockerill, *The Epistle to the Hebrews*, 16–17; DeSilva, *Perseverance in Gratitude*, 16; ibid, *The Letter to the Hebrews in Social Scientific Perspective*, 50.

[40] Homi Bhabha, *The Location of Culture* (London: Routledge, 1994), 9.

Bhabha—commenting on Franz Fanon's *Black Skin, White Masks*—rightly so, diaspora existence is hybrid in nature because the space between the diaspora land and home land is not clear-cut.[41] Such a hybrid space ("dissembling image of being in at least two places at the same time")[42] is a subversive and disturbing distance because it challenges 'othering', "forced-assimilations, cultural mimicry, internalized self-rejection, and displacement. This hybrid space is otherwise known as 'hyphens' where people live.

The author of Hebrews proposes 'Melchizedek tradition' in the Old Testament. Abraham crosses the border and gives tithes to a Canaanite king-priest of Salem, as a political tool to re-invent the so-called 'margins' themselves where people are being pushed to and a strategy to (re)read the scriptures. This reconceptualizes the 'centers' that create 'margins' and embrace 'otherness' of the 'margins' as a rhetorical site of liberation and resistance. The basic premise of such a strategy is contextualization, which, for Segovia, implies two characteristics—'otherness' and 'engagement'.[43] In so doing, as with any cross-cultural encounter of and political engagement with the ancient text, irrespective of whether it is an "emic description" or "etic description," the author's interpretation of the Melchizedek tradition in the epistle might have some kind of ethnocentric allusions or remarks, wittingly or unwittingly.

The Melchizedek Tradition and Jesus' High Priesthood: Re-imagining Christology

There are primarily two immediate reasons why the audience of Hebrews re-imagine a new christology:

1. The Levitical priesthood is exclusive and antiquated as it is territorial and centralized (7:11-14).
2. They believe that Christ fulfilled the Torah and all that is envisaged in it for the salvation of humanity. Therefore,

[41] Homi Bhabha, "Remembering Fanon: Self, Psyche and the Colonial Condition," in *Colonial Discourse and Postcolonial Theory: A Reader* (eds., P. Williams and L. Chrisman; New York: Columbia University Press, 1994), 112–23, here117.

[42] Bhabha, "Remembering Fanon," 117.

[43] Segovia, "Toward a Hermeneutics of the Diaspora," 58–59.

> as followers of Christ, the audience of Hebrew too stand in historical and soteriological continuity with Jewish heritage. But, Jewish leaders located them 'outside' the orbit of Judaism(s).

Hebrews identifies a new de-territorialized priesthood in Jesus which defines margins as 'rhetorical space' that transcends place and territory. This the author achieves by linking Jesus' priesthood with his divine sonship to the priesthood of Melchizedek. But, it poses certain important questions. Why does the author present Jesus as the high priest over against the Levitical priesthood, not a king or an emperor over the Roman emperors? Is it simply a matter of exchanging the superiority (supersessionism) of the Levitical priesthood for that of Jesus? How does it foster the geopolitical liberation (Segovia) of the audience of the letter? Can the priesthood of Jesus function as a liberating symbol, breaking through power relations insisted upon by religious orthodoxies? Answering these questions would tell us about how the re-imagination of christology in Hebrews becomes the political praxis of the marginalized and hyphenated audience.

Re-imagination of Christology: A Geopolitical Resistance

The new re-imagination of christology engages the diaspora audience of the epistle in various ways.

First, Jesus' high priesthood according to the order of Melchizedek destabilizes the so-called centrality of the 'sacred center' (altar) that creates 'sacred boundaries' by separating "holy land" from the 'waste land;' instead it envisages multiplicity of altars. Diaspora people cannot relate to the territoriality of Levitical priesthood and that of God's promises. They need a new priesthood that is not territory based and altar centered. It is in Jesus that the author and his/her readers find a new de-territorialized and de-genealogical priest.

To validate the new de-territorialized and de-genealogical priesthood of Jesus, the author extensively uses Melchizedek tradition. Abraham, the father of the nations, tithes to a Canaanite priest and received blessings from him. If Abraham, the forbearer Levi, accepts the priesthood of Melchizedek, who is not even a Jew, Jesus can also be accepted as a priest. More importantly, Jesus is the son of God. But, while accepting the priesthood of Melchizedek, Abraham proposes a new understanding of God. For Abraham, the God of Melchizedek, 'God of Most High' (*El Elyon*), is characteristically linked to places and natural phenomenon, which means they are static and fixed (see also *El-Roi*-Gen 16:13; *El Elyon*-Gen 14:18). In contrast, for Abraham, his God is a de-territorialized and 'detranscendentalized' God who cannot be knotted to any territory but to people and communities. The understanding of a journeying God is further evident in the sojourner or pilgrim motif (4:11; 13:1–7). To reinforce the understanding of journeying God further, Hebrews employs the term tabernacle instead of the word temple. The same tradition can be found further in the Exodus tradition: Moses pitched a tabernacle outside the tent when he speaks face to face with God (Exod 33:7-11). It reflects the paradox of sovereignty; sovereignty is inside and outside at the same time.

In Hebrews, Jesus' priesthood is interpreted in view of the Yom Kippur than the Passover festivals, as in the gospels. Sacrificial animals are killed outside the sacred boundaries, but only blood is brought inside the tent (Lev 16:12, 15; 17:3). 'Outside the tent' is a place where one find those who are ritually impure (Lev 24:14, 23; Num 15:36), especially lepers (Num 5:2; 12:14); the defiled wait outside the tent for purification (Num 12:14-15; 31:19-20); law breakers executed outside the tent (Num 15:32–36); it is a place associated with Death (Deut 2:4), especially by stoning (Lev 24:14, 23; Num 15:36). The author draws parallel between Jesus' death outside the city gate of the 'holy city,' Jerusalem (13:11), and the disposal of the 'impure' bodies of the Yom Kippur sacrificial victims and the ritually impure. The letter also associates this boundary crossing imagery with the believers' anticipated, eschatological city (13:14). And thus, argues that this 'permeable boundaries' define the new ontology of the diaspora community with de-centered altars which positions itself in relation to a God, who in Jesus became a victim by himself, is with the victims on the hyphens.

Second, Hebrews' provocative re-imagination of christology is a geopolitical praxis in many respects. Melchizedek (Gen 14:18–24) may be linked with Zadok, the later priest of David (2 Sam 8:17;

1 Kings 1:8–12), if "Salem" (Gen 14:18) is an early reference to Jerusalem. If so, it can be argued that David must have used the Melchizedek tradition to validate his political agenda of centralizing religious power and political power in Jerusalem. This explains the formation of Ps 110:4. But, the author of Hebrews uses the same Melchizedek tradition to expose how liturgical systems were ab/used to territorialize Jewish cultic practices during the time of Davidic monarchy.

Furthermore, Herod replaced the Hasmoneans with foreign Jewish priestly families from Babylon (that of Hananel) and Egypt (beginning with Jesus son of Phiabi, then Simon son of Boethus) and Jerusalem (Matthias son of Theophilus) [Josephus, *Ant.* 15:18–22, 40–41, 51–56, 319–322; 17:78, 161–167]. The consequence of it was a weakened priesthood, now appointed by the imperial political authority. Because these new priestly families lacked legitimacy, they collaborated with Herodian dynasty and Roman imperial regimes. But, the letter to the Hebrews out rightly disavows the empire nominated/appointed priests by re-imagining Jesus as their eternal high priest. They rejected not only the authority of the Roman empire to appoint priests in Jerusalem but the empire itself.

Third, with regard to the question of supersessionism in Hebrews, the superiority of Jesus cult over the 'inferior' cult of Israel challenges (though discreetly) the contemporary imperial cult such as the Capitoline cult and other imperial cults associated with it.[44] Hebrews does it in the context of the Roman emperors twice having to rebuild the temple of Jupiter after its destruction by fire with the money extracted from the Jerusalem temple tax (*fiscus Judiacus)* to the Capitoline treasury.[45]

Fourth, in Hebrews, we find multiple supersessionist claims intertwined. The superior cult of Jesus contests not only the claims

---

[44] A group of three deities—Jupiter, Juno and Minerva (The *Capitoline Triad*)—were worshipped in ancient Roman religion in temples known as *Capitolia* on Rome's Capitoline Hill (Latin *Capitolium*).

[45] *Fiscus Judaicus* ("Jewish tax") was a tax that the Jews had to pay to the temple of the Roman supreme god Jupiter after the destruction of their own temple in 70 CE. See Ellen Bradshaw Aitken, "Reading Hebrews in Flavian Rome," *USQR* 59/3-4 (2005), 82-85.

of Levitical priesthood appointed by the empire but also that of the Capitoline city itself.[46] Unlike the Capitoline (*imperium*), the new community (*basiliea*-12:28) constituted outside the "sacred boundaries" is not a city (13:11-14). Hebrews' position on the precariousness of the city is an explicit criticism of the Roman city culture. To reinforce the volatility of the imperial city claims, Hebrews proposes the term 'sojourner' to re-constitute the identity of the members of the new community with porous boundaries as opposed to the term 'citizen.' The new *basiliea* on the margins, of the marginalized and by the marginalized is unshaken because it has no margins or center. Fixity of both the centre and the margins is only an illusion. Such a socio-political proposition perfectly fits into the diasporic/marginal experience of the audience.

Fifth, the use of Melchizedek tradition in Hebrews proves that hermeneutical activity is a political praxis. The author of Hebrews uses same tradition which King David used to reinforce his imperial and political agenda as a hermeneutical tool to interrogate the imperial cultic ideology. As students of the Bible, it is our responsibility to see that the biblical traditions that we uphold, including the supersessionist traditions and claims, do not become the repertoire of empire but vehicle of subversive liturgical discourse of critique of empire and its cultic ideology.

Sixth, the transaction between Abraham and Melchizedek opens up the possibility of a new way of engaging the borders and negotiating the "structures of power built on differences" (Sugirtharajah). Both Abraham and Melchizedek were not suffering from xenophobia; instead they were hyphenating with each other by positioning themselves in a radical relation to each other ('Planetarity').[47] For Abraham and Melchizedek, the physical/geographical boundaries are not lines of division that neatly divide one from the other, but always a 'site of hybridity'/'liminality' (Homi Bhabha) and 'elusive zones' of negotiation.

---

[46] Aitken, "Reading Hebrews in Flavian Rome," 82-85.

[47] In her book *Death of a Discipline* (2003), Spivak proposes the idea of a 'planetarity' as an ethical alternative to globalization. It aims to overwrite the globe as it is made up of lines of latitude and longitude. The planet, on the other hand, is concrete and ecological.

Such spatial practices envisage a non-territorial spatiality ("nomadic spatiality"). Though Abraham and Melchizedek had geographical and political boundaries/territories, their understanding of territory was different from "sedentary territory," which views land as a fixed plane.[48] For Abraham and Melchizedek, "nomadic spatiality" does not parcel out a space to people; nomads are localized but delimited.[49] Therefore, one cannot find any conflict between "home land" and 'borderland' in the transactions of Abraham and Melchizedek because they re-imagined space in such a way that it transcends place and boundaries.

Conclusion

By going outside the tent, Jesus the high priest according to the order of Melchizedek also engages in a new nomadic spatial practice, which calls for a new "politics of location." The author of Hebrews invites his readers for such a praxeological re-imagination of christology and spatiality so as to challenge the marginality of the margin and the centrality of the center and thereby politically transform and transfigure their marginality and 'hyphenality' as privileged fields of encounter and as dialogical and deconstructive space. Such a transfigured experiencing of spatiality will ensure that the audience of the epistle experience their time in diaspora as the "time of the end" ("messianic time"), where one is invited to experience *eschaton* in history, in relation to "the end of time" ("apocalyptic time") or eternity.

[48] 'Sedentary territory' is defined by its borders and governed by authorities.

[49] 'Nomadic spatiality' or 'the spatial logic of the nomads' is not based on regularity or predictability because it does not fix or enclosed spaces. It "de-territorializes and opens-up spaces characterized by random movements."

Chapter 6

"Justification by Faith Alone" (*Sola fide*) Towards an *Ekklēsia* of the Multitude?

"When the world tightens its fist, be water"
(Tshombe Sekou)

Introduction

The primary texts for the European Renaissance were the works of Greek and Roman writers. For the Reformation, however, only one text mattered: the Bible. In theological terms, it is not too much to claim that Luther's discovery of "the doctrine of justification by grace through faith alone," often shortened to "justification by faith" (*sola fide*), actually lit up the fires of the Reformation in the 16th century Europe. For Luther, *sola fide* means that God accepts the wicked as they are, and starts renewing them from there.[1] This paper attempts to examine if the Protestant talk of "justification by faith alone" has more to say to contemporary socio-political needs and ekklēsiological concerns than has been generally recognized.

[1] "But to one who without works trusts him who justifies the ungodly, such faith is reckoned as righteousness." (Rom 4:5 NRSV).

Medieval Christendom: The Antipode of Democracy and Secularism?

As in the Greek-speaking world of classical antiquity, Aristotle's distinction between two basic human faculties of *poiesis* (production or labour, the foundation of the household and economy, in its etymological sense) and *praxis* (action as intersubjective exchange, the foundation of politics, the city, and commerce) was understood to be embodied in all fundamental socio-political institutions in the Middle Ages,[2] including the church. While *poiesis* comprised the realm of the household (*oikos*), praxis comprised the civic order. The former included the realm of production for the sustenance of life (*economy or oeconomia*). And the latter comprised courts, military, and government (*politics or politia*), which was somewhat the exclusive prerogative of the aristocracy.

In the Middle Ages, a third institution called *ekklēsia* was added to the two fundamental institutions—*oeconomia* and *politia*. Together, these three institutions formed an organic hegemony called *corpus christianum*. Since the body of christendom (*corpus christianum*) had papacy at its head, the papal see could not only exercise primacy over the government and the secular affairs of the empire but also centralize religious and political powers in papacy. As a result, the church, as represented by papal see, had become the center of civic order and political life, to the extent of even possessing the right to appoint kings and rulers.

This "unholy" nexus between religion and state was sustained for centuries by the "Donation of Constantine" (*Donatio Constantini* and *Constitutum Constantini*), the document purporting to record the Roman emperor Constantine's bestowal of vast territory and spiritual and temporal power on Pope Sylvester I (reigned 314–335) and his successors.[3] Leo IX (1049–54) was the first pope to cite it

---

[2] Ruth Mohl, *The Three Estates in Medieval and Renaissance Literature* (New York: Columbia University Press, 1933), 10ff.

[3] The Donation was based on the *Legenda S. Silvestri* (Latin: "The Legend of St. Sylvester"), a 5th-century account of the relationship between Pope Sylvester I and the emperor Constantine. It begins with the tale of the conversion of Constantine to christianity after Sylvester I miraculously cured him of leprosy. Constantine then

as an authority in an official act, and subsequent popes used it in their struggles with the Roman emperors and other secular leaders. Various ecclesiastics included it in their codes of canon law, and even Rome's opponents seldom questioned its authenticity.

The European church controlled the colossal mineral wealth in Germany, which led to papal exploitation. The popes continued to make money by the sale of indulgences. The church became chief exploiter and tyrant. The common people hated the popes with their religious and political structure, and the nobles and the clergy who concentrated in the feudal power. Other economic factors can be seen in the nobility's refusal to allow peasants to hunt when unable to grow sufficient food.

The Donation had great influence on the political and religious life in medieval Europe, until it was clearly demonstrated to be a forgery by the Italian humanist Lorenzo Valla. In 1440 Lorenzo Valla showed that the Latin used in the document was not that of the 4th century. At the dawn of Reformation, Luther had read Valla's refutation and convinced other reformers that the document was the forgery of the Antichrist embodied by the one seated on the papal throne.[4] This caused in an unprecedented revolt against European clericalism, Papal tyranny and Roman Catholic magisterium.

Numerous 'reform' efforts predated Martin Luther's nailing of 95 theses on Wittenberg Castle church's door on October 31, 1517. The pressure for reform within the Roman Catholic church is probably as old as Roman Catholicism itself. But, the outburst of 1517 as caused by the new alliance of religion and state, as represented by the iron-willed Machiavellian power-despots like

---

declares the importance of Rome to the church because it is the city of the apostles Peter and Paul. The second section of the forgery contains the actual donation: Constantine, in preparing to depart to his new capital of Constantinople, bestows upon the pope supremacy over the sees of Antioch, Alexandria, Constantinople, and Jerusalem and all the world's churches. He next grants administrative rights to Sylvester and his successors over estates granted to churches throughout the empire. Most importantly, Constantine gives the pope control of the imperial palace in Rome and all the regions of the Western Empire; this effectively conveys the notion that the pope has the right to appoint secular rulers in the West.

[4] Heiko Oberman, *Luther: Man between God and the Evil* (New York: Image, 1992), 42.

Pope Leo X (1513–1521) and his predecessor Julius II (1503–1513), and bourgeois respectively.

The famines of 1315–17 and the Black Death in Europe killed thousands. Then, too, craft guilds and secret societies grew. Some of these were disguised evangelical circles. Other guilds and societies called for societal change and communal living. The movements like *Brethren of the Common Life*, which stressed mystical experience and subjectivism, attempted some renewal among mainstream Catholics. But, on the whole, every single movement was suppressed by massacre initiated by Inquisition and implemented by the Lords, especially the French Peasants Revolt in 1320 and the English Peasant's Revolt in 1381,[5] which were directed against the feudal aristocracy and the land-rich church institutions. In 1209, a sect called the "Poor Men of Lyons" in Southern France, which practised a life according to the Bible, was massacred as they were regarded as enemies of the church, and later in the crusades.[6]

This explains why Luther's primary concern was to dismantle *corpus christianum*, and thus to secularize politics and democratize religion. With the same intention, he put forth his famous distinction of the two regimes—"two kingdoms doctrines." While not rejecting the distinction between the spiritual and the secular, he emphasized the distinctions of the three institutions —the household (*oeconomia)*, the public realm (*politia)*, and the church (*ekklēsia)*— and their groundings as God's mandate. Luther deconstructed the three states by stressing their uniqueness. He did not identify the *ekklēsia* either with *corpus christianum* or with the spiritual regime; instead Luther demystified *ekklēsia* and regarded it as an earthly institution as much as the civil government and economy (domain of the household). However, for Luther, *ekklēsia* is the first institution given to humanity: "Here we have the establishment of the church

---

[5] D. H. Lawrence, *Movements in European History* (Oxford: Oxford University Press, 1971), 169ff.

[6] Lawrence, *Movements in European History*, 170ff.

(*ekklēsia*) before there was any government of the home (*oeconomia*) and of the state (*politia*)."[7]

By dismantling the *corpus christianum*, Luther secularized *ekklēsia* and democratized its faith, but without undermining the unique character of the other two estates—(*oeconomia)*, the public realm (*politia)*. In this respect, the Protestant Reformation paved the way for (European version of) secularism and liberalism. More importantly, Reformation movement broke the grip of papal dictatorship and the despotism of the medieval European christendom. It is against this larger context that we need to position Luther's interpretation of Paul's idea of "justification by faith" and how/why it turned out to be an 'occupy church' movement of the 16th century.

Justification by faith as Demystification of *Ekklēsia*: Occupy "Treasury of Merit" and Purgatory Movement?

Martin Luther was a devoted monk of the Augustinian order and a devoted teacher. He was deeply affected by the unhealthy alliance between papacy (religion) and state, papal corruption and economic manipulation, empty formalism, clericalism and commercialization of religious practices. The problem lay in his own spiritual life; he had no quietness of conscience. The doctrine of human sinfulness depressed him, and no amount of penance and confession seemed able to remove his own sense of guilt before God. What Luther feared most of all was "the justice of God." By this he understood the anger and judgment of God against the sinners. Luther had problems with the Medieval church's understanding of God as judge; the whole life on earth was but a preparation for the final judgment.

For Luther realized that he had been misled by the Catholic teaching of justification, particularly its teaching on indulgences. This was the belief, promoted by the papal authority, that saints who have excess merit than what they need, which is called "condign merit" (*meritum de condigno*), which is as high as supererogatory merit, had built up their surplus merit with God in "the treasury of merits."

[7] Martin Luther, *Lectures on Genesis*, *Chapters 1–5* (ed., Jaroslav Pelikan; Saint Louis, Missouri: Concordia, 1958), 103.

It is distinguished from "congruous merit" (*meritum de congruo*) or appropriate merit. Since the church has the keys of "the treasury of surplus," Pope could mystically transfer merit from "the treasury of merits" to individual ('indulgence'), upon financial contribution to the church or by pilgrimage to Rome. Such supernatural transfer of merit ensured remission of sins entirely or time spent by the sinful christian in purgatory.

Sometime in 1515 or 1516, Luther discovered that only scripture (*sola scriptura*), not tradition, should be the source of faith and practices of the church. The programmatic text that drove Luther to take his radical stand was Romans 1:17: "For in it the righteousness of God is revealed through faith for faith; as it is written, 'The one who is righteous will live by faith'" (NRSV). This discovery was obviously a critical shift in his understanding of God. He realized that God's justice in no way justifies handing the keys of so-called purgatory and the treasury of merits to the papal see. This tremendous liberative grasp of the gospel was indeed good news for the countless thousands who were terrified of hell, dismayed by the prospects of purgatory and treasury of surplus merits, and put off by the abusive liturgical practices of the Medieval church. For Luther, christianity starts from the subversive offer of unconditional grace extended to all, and not rooted in *corpus christianum* or the mystical powers of the papal see. This revelatory discovery turned out to be a resistance movement, demystifying the *ekklēsia* and occupying the purgatory and "the treasury of merits."

Luther believed that Paul was attacking Jewish legalism, which maintained that one's standing before God, one's righteousness, was grounded on careful observance of the Law. Luther used his interpretation of Paul, especially Romans 1:17, to attack Catholicism of his time and the popular belief that one could work out one's own salvation by doing the works of the Torah. According to Luther, for Paul, justification of the individual was by faith in Christ 'alone' (*allein*), not by fulfilling the requirements of the Torah;[8] "therefore

[8] Martin Luther, "The Freedom of a Christian," in *Three Treatises* (trans. W. A. Lambert; Philadelphia: Fortress, 1970), 280–81; idem, "Preface to the Epistle of St Paul to the Romans," in *Martin Luther: Selections from His Writings* (ed., John Dillenberger; Garden City, NY: Doubleday, 1961), 22.

this is a marvellous definition of christian righteousness, for the sake of our faith in Christ or for the sake of Christ."[9] It is what he called a *justitia alienum*, an alien righteousness; a righteousness that belongs properly to somebody else. It is a righteousness that is *extra nos*, meaning outside of us. Namely, the righteousness of Christ.

Luther disagreed with the Roman Catholics on the issue of whether God in justifying the individuals makes them just or righteous, or counts them as righteous. According to the traditional Protestants, righteousness is imputed to those who believe in Christ; justification means a divine declaration stressing the stream of law-court imagery, based on the merits of Christ.[10] For Luther, Pauline idea of "justification by faith" has nothing to do with human achievement; it is the very opposite of doing the "works of the Law" in order to earn acceptance of God. Faith is simply the acceptance of God's offer to accept as we are, which is rooted in his restorative justice. To derive a "declarative interpretation of justification,"[11] Luther used the Greek word that was in the New Testament, not the Latin word. The words *dikaios* (δικαιος) and *dikaiosune* (δικαιοσύνη) mean to *regard* or to *count* or to *declare* as righteous.

Roman Catholics teach justification but fundamentally as a sacerdotal matter. They followed a "behavioral interpretation of justification"[12] which insists that righteousness is *imparted* to those who believe in Christ, which sees justification as a divine *transformation*, stressing covenantal and ethical streams;[13] it is a divine action which actually transforms the one who believes (*grace infused*). The Latin word for justification that was used at this time in church history was *justificare*—and it's the word from which we get the English word *justification*. It came from the Roman judicial system. And the term *justificare* is made up of the word *justus*, which

---

[9] Martin Luther, *Lectures on Galatians, Chapters 1–4* (ed., Jaroslav Pelikan; St Louis, Missouri: Concordia, 1964), 233.

[10] Luther, *Lectures on Galatians, Chapters 1–4*, 137.

[11] Anthony C. Thiselton, *The Living Paul: An Introduction to the Apostle's Life and Thought* (Downers Grove, Illinois: IVP Academic, 2009), 92–93.

[12] Thiselton, *The Living Paul*, 92–93.

[13] Michael J. Gorman, *Reading Paul* (Eugene, Oregon: Cascade, 2008), 115.

is justice or righteousness, and the verb *facare*, which means to make. And so, the Catholic church understood justification as what happens when God makes unrighteous people righteous.

Justification by Faith Alone (*Sola fide*): Did Luther (Completely?) Misread Paul?

Luther's understanding of "justification by grace through faith alone" still resonates strongly and speaks powerfully to the self-indulgent and self-righteous of our time. But, in spelling out his discovery into "justification by faith alone," Luther made many assumptions, which can now be seen to be mistaken:

1. Luther was right to see Paul's conversion experience at the threshold of Damascus as a key to interpret Paul's concept of justification by faith; Damascus theophany is an experience of 'inner conversion' and thus entails a change of religion from Judaism to christianity. In Dunn's view, rightly so, Luther failed to see the character of Paul's conversion: "what he [Paul] was converted *from*, and what he was converted *to*" [emphasis added].[14] Paul's conversion is *from* his earlier life in Judaism as a violent persecutor of the church of God (Gal 1:13; 1 Cor 15:8–9) due to his excessive zeal (Phil 3:6) *to* the gentiles.[15] Paul's 'conversion' is not about relieving his guilt-consciousness or coming to realize that keeping the Torah fosters self-righteousness and Jewish legalism. To be more precise, Paul never speaks of his experience of conversion as a 'conversion,' but as a 'calling' or 'commissioning' (Gal 1:15–16; 1 Cor 9:1–2; 15:8–10).
2. Luther misread Paul's own self-testimony and of the Judaism within which Paul grew up. He regarded the Judaism of Paul's day as a narrow legalistic religion. This is implicitly or explicitly anti-Semitic as it identifies 'works' and the 'law' with Judaism. As a result, Luther interpreted Paul's understanding of "justification by faith" as opposed to the "works of the Law." The

[14] James D. G. Dunn and Alan M. Suggate, *The Justice of God: A Fresh Look at the Old Doctrine of Justification of Faith* (Grand Rapids, Michigan: Eerdmans, 1993), 22.

[15] Dunn and Suggate, *The Justice of God*, 24.

trouble with this depiction of Judaism is that it made no sense to those Jews who bothered themselves with justification as it is not novum of christianity but having the character of a Midrash and thus a Jewish notion,[16] as Gal 2:15–16 unmistakably shows.[17] And in Gal 5:3, Paul discusses justification in relation to a Halakah. This implies the Hebrew/Jewish understanding of 'righteousness' *(δικαιοσύνη),* which entails a relational concept as it is broader than 'forgiveness' rather than a legal one.[18] The term encompasses the obligations of someone who is part of a relationship.

3. For Luther, Paul used justification by faith primarily to attack Jewish legalism, which maintained that one's standing before God was grounded on the careful observance of the Law.[19] Luther used his interpretation of Paul to challenge Catholicism of his day and the popular belief that one could earn salvation by one's own efforts: for Luther's Paul, justification of the individual was by faith in Christ, not by carrying out the requirements of the Law. All of this is a serious misunderstanding of what Paul meant by "justification" and "works of the law" for various reasons.

   First, perhaps due to the discovery of the Dead Sea Scrolls and the Vatican II council, over the last few decades the traditional Protestant interpretation of Pauline theology, especially his justification by faith, has been repudiated. Though Krister Stendahl and W. D. Davies had already been pointing in a

---

[16] James D. G. Dunn, *Theology of Paul the Apostle* (Grand Rapids, Michigan: Eerdmans, 1998), 30–44; Dunn and Suggate, *The Justice of God*, 17; Peter J. Tomson, *Paul and the Jewish: Halakha in the Letters of the Apostle to the Gentiles* (Minneapolis: Fortress, 1990), 66–68.

[17] Richard B. Hays, *The Conversion of the Imagination: Paul as Interpreter of Israel's Scripture* (Grand Rapids, Michigan: Eerdmans, 2005), 71.

[18] Kathy Ehrensperger, *That We May be Mutually Encouraged: Feminism and the New Perspective in Pauline Studies* (New York: T&T Clark, 2004), 150; Thiselton, *The Living Paul*, 92.

[19] Thomas R. Schreiner, *Paul, Apostle of God's Glory in Christ: A Pauline Theology* (Downers Grove, Illinois: InterVarsity, 2001), 118–23

similar direction,[20] E. P. Sanders' ground breaking work *Paul and Palestinian Judaism* in 1977 primarily accounts for this volte-face, better known as 'new perspective on Paul',[21] later championed by James D. G. Dunn and N. T. Wright. According to Sanders, with the exception of 4 Ezra, Israel's covenant relation to God is basic to Second Temple Judaism ('covenantal nomism'):[22] in the Old Testament and in the later Jewish writings, obedience to the Law is not understood as a means of *entering* ('getting in') the covenant, or of *attaining* that special relationship with God; in Jewish self-understanding, the Law had been given by God as part of the choice of Israel. And, therefore, carrying out the requirements of the Law *maintains* ('staying in') one's position in the covenant, but it does not *earn* God's grace as such. This 'theology of election' is a theme which is constantly referred to in the Jewish Scriptures (Deut 7:6).

Second, Paul criticizes the Law (a) in so far as some (whether Jews, or Christ-believing Jews) try to impose requirements of the Law on the so-called gentile believers rather than acknowledge them as full sharers in the promise to Abraham and the people of God, and (b) in so far as it causes divisions between Jews and the gentiles in Jesus movement. Paul continues to uphold the validity of the Torah.

Third, as Dunn fittingly argues, Paul seems to develop his understanding of justification by faith in the light of his dispute with Peter at Antioch as reflected in Gal 2:16, and carefully restated later in Romans 3–4.[23] This indicates, while providing a

---

[20] Krister Stendahl, *Paul Among Jews and Gentiles and Other Essays* (Philadelphia: Fortress, 1976); W. D. Davies, *Paul and Rabbinic Judaism: Some Rabbinic Elements in Pauline Theology* (4th edn.; Philadelphia: Fortress, 1980).

[21] Dunn has often been regarded as the one who coined the term. See "The New Perspective on Paul," *BJRL* 65 (1983), 95–122. But according to Dunn, Wright used the phrase earlier in 1978: "The Paul of History and the Apostle of Faith," *Tyndale Bulletin* 29 (1978), 61, 64, 77–78.

[22] E. P. Sanders, *Paul and Palestinian Judaism* (Philadelphia: Fortress, 1977); idem, *Paul, the Law, and the Jewish People* (Minneapolis: Fortress, 1983), 20.

[23] Graham N. Stanton, "Paul's Gospel," in *The Cambridge Companion to St Paul* (ed., James D. G. Dunn; Cambridge: Cambridge University Press, 2003),

fundamental statement of human dependence on God, that Paul presents the doctrine primarily vis-à-vis gentile acceptability, and more fundamentally, human acceptability by God.

4. Luther clearly overlooked the recurrent ethnic dimension of the apostle's reasoning when he juxtaposes Jews and gentiles in the passages where he is discussing Moses' Law and the issues the Law raised in his mission to the gentiles.[24] The Jews had treated the Law as a boundary marker and had not recognized that the scripture had anticipated the inclusion of the gentiles. Paul responds that the boundary marking God's people is not circumcision, Sabbath or any other "works of the Law" (ἔργα νόμου), but rather an existence 'in Christ.'[25] In contending that "works of the Law" necessarily includes the notion of boundaries, Dunn correctly observes that one can find such indications in the corresponding phrase in Qumran Writings especially 4 QMMT.[26] Whenever Paul speaks positively of the Law, it is the Law understood apart from Jewish ethnic identity; Paul interprets the Law in new light.[27] Whenever Paul speaks negatively of the Law, his purpose is to identify these ethnic boundary markers or works of the Law. In other words, the fundamental problem Paul has with the Law does not stem from a pessimistic anthropology in which humans are unable to accomplish the demands of the Law.

173–184, here 180; idem, Dunn, *Theology of Paul*, 372.

[24] A. Andrew Das, "Paul and the Law: Pressure points in the Debate," in *Paul Unbound: Other Perspectives on the Apostle* (ed., Mark D. Given; Grand Rapids, Michigan: Baker Academic, 2010), 99–116, here 103-104.

[25] Das, "Paul and the Law," 104.

[26] Das, "Paul and the Law," 106; Jason Maston and Aaron Sherwood, "4QMMT and Romans 3:21–31," in *Reading Romans in Context: Paul and Second Temple Judaism* (eds., Ben C. Blackwell, John K. Goodrich, and Jason Maston; Grand Rapids, Michigan: Zondervan, 2015), 52–58, here 55–57.

[27] Marvin R. Wilson, *Our Father Abraham: Jewish Roots of the Christian Faith* (Grand Rapids, Michigan: Eerdmans, 1989), 28–29; David Wenham, *Paul: Follower of Jesus or Founder of Christianity?* (Grand Rapids, Michigan: Eerdmans, 1995), 54; Udo Schnelle, *Apostle Paul: His Life and Theology* (trans., M. Eugene Boring; Grand Rapids, Michigan: Baker Academic, 2003), 300.

5. The traditional Protestant interpretation of justification by faith tends to focus on the inner beings of the individuals as if justification constituted an affair for the individual. But, Paul's primary concerns, precisely in the language of justification, are public, covenantal, and corporate because, as 'new perspective' rightly contends, Paul positions justification in the context of Jew-gentile relationship.[28]
6. Luther's doctrine of justification, while rooted in the death and resurrection of Jesus, overlooked the relational nature of the doctrine and its interaction with social justice. The result is that the social dimension of Paul's message, especially of his justification by faith, is left to divisive forces, often with disastrous consequences.

Luther shaped his reading of Paul's understanding of justification by faith in the larger context of the growing unrest and protest among christians against the *corpus christianum*. To dismantle the empire-papacy unholy alliance, achieved primarily through the "Donation of Constantine," and thus to separate religion and state, Luther resorts to the doctrine of *sola scriptura* ("by scripture alone"), especially Pauline concept of justification by faith. To a great extent, despite the limitations in Luther's reading of Paul, as explained above, Luther's resistance movement succeeded in secularizing politics and uncentering *ekklēsia*.

However, of all the critical issues implicitly or explicitly embedded in his interpretation, a few of Luther's vital errors became extremely crucial and fatal. Luther completely overlooked the issue of ethnicity, covenant, election, and the Law, and its implications for Jew-gentile relationship in Pauline churches. Moreover, Paul's positive statements about his earlier life in Judaism and his high regard for the Law were also not taken into account; he misread

---

[28] Douglas Harink, *Paul among the Postliberals: Pauline Theology beyond Christendom and Modernity* (Eugene, Oregon: Wipe & Stock, 2003), 56, 59; John Howard Yoder, *The Politics of Jesus: Vicit Agnus Noster* (2nd edn; Grand Rapids, Michigan: Eerdmans, 1994 [1972], 212–227; Thiselton, *The Living Paul*, 97; Michael J. Gorman, *Inhabiting the Cruciform God: Kenosis, Justification, and Theosis in Paul's Narrative Soteriology*, (Grand Rapids, Michigan: Eerdmans, 2009), 70; Gorman, *Reading Paul*, 116.

Judaism as a narrow legalistic religion. Luther reduced justification by faith as Paul formulated to individual salvation as though that was all there was to it.

Consequently, as Derrida accurately contends,[29] "it is Luther whose anti-Semitism provided the template for *Mein Kampf*"—a 1925 autobiographical book by Adolf Hitler, which outlines his political ideology and future plans for Germany.[30] Luther also failed to see the connection between justification by faith and God's justice. This explains why Luther justified the actions of the Princes against the serfs, even when it involves acts of brutal violence, in his piece *Against the Murderous, Thieving Hordes of Peasants* (*Wider die Mordischen und Reubischen Rotten der Bawren*) related to the German Peasant's War. Luther, who is often considered to be the foundation for the peasant's revolt, even venerates those who fight against the peasants, stating that "anyone who is killed fighting on the side of the rulers may be a true martyr in the eyes of God." While all these issues are pertinent enough to be continuously grilled, it is perhaps equally important, if not more, that we revisit Paul's "justification by faith" as we celebrate the 500th anniversary of Lutheran Reformation. There are still sufficient subversive theological resources left within Paul's understanding of justification of faith that can provide an impetus for *re*-forming Reformation itself and making it an ongoing liberative event.

Justification by Faith: Envisioning the *Ekklēsia* of Multitude

Perhaps the most persuasive way to uncover the subversive dimensions of justification by faith is not only to identify how Paul positions his idea and where he hangs on it but also to revisit them. Very often the scholars of both Paulinism and Lutheranism closely connect justification by faith to the belief about the death and resurrection of Jesus; God accepts the sinners because Jesus' death makes satisfaction before God for the sins of the people. While this being a very vital

[29] Theodore W. Jennings, Jr., *Reading Derrida/Thinking Paul* (Stanford, California: Stanford University Press, 2006), 156.

[30] *Mein Kampf* is a 1925 autobiographical book by Adolf Hitler. The work outlines Hitler's political ideology and future plans for Germany.

emphasis for Paul, he connects justification by faith also to Abraham and christian baptism. But, this crucial positioning is either ignored or not sufficiently highlighted, both among Pauline and Lutheran scholars.

Justification by faith is Paul's protest not as an individual sinner against excessive Jewish legalism, but as an apostle to the gentile against Jewish exclusivism and ethnic nationalism. Paul achieves at such a theological position by linking his apostolic mission to the gentiles to the original promise to a concrete historical personage, Abraham: "in you [Abraham] all the families of the earth shall be blessed" (Gen 12:3 NRSV). It is this insight that lies at the heart of his exposition in Galatians 3–4 and Romans 3–4, and 9–11. This explains why Paul saw Israel's calling to be "as a light to the nations, that my salvation may reach to the end of the earth" (Isa 49:6 NRSV),[31] which stood behind Paul's conviction that he must now help to fulfill that role (Acts 13:47).[32]

Therefore, Paul's negative references to 'the works of the Law' were not to do with attaining righteousness by observing the Law, but refers to Jewish insistence that gentile converts must come under the 'boundary markers' of Israel. For Paul, when gentiles believe in Christ, they become part of the covenant community "not by virtue of physical descent from him but by virtue of sharing his trust in the God who made the promises to Abraham."[33] In this way, Paul justifies ethnic groupings of Jews and gentiles, and rejects narrow Jewish ethnic nationalism and its 'rigid sacred boundaries.'

By resisting the forces of Jewish ethnic nationalism, Paul envisions a new *ekklēsia* which embraces the otherness of the gentiles/'others' and welcomes people with different ethnic

---

[31] "It is too light a thing that you should be my servant to raise up the tribes of Jacob and to restore the survivors of Israel; I will give you as a light to the nations, that my salvation may reach to the end of the earth" (Isa 49:6 NRSV).

[32] "For so the Lord has commanded us, saying, 'I have set you to be a light for the Gentiles, so that you may bring salvation to the ends of the earth'" (Act 13:47 NRSV).

[33] Hays, *The Conversion of the Imagination*, 73–74.

backgrounds, which Hardt and Negri would call 'the multitude:'[34] the *ekklēsia* of the multitude.[35] For Paul, the new ethnic groupings not only challenge the rigid/sacred boundaries that exclude people but also conceptualize a democratic, inclusive and participatory space. In the words of Hardt and Negri, "The multitude is composed of radical differences, singularities, that never be synthesized in an identity."[36] The multitude revisits and interrogates religion and the space that religion is supposed to inhabit. Thus, it aims to create a physical and imaginary space so that an alternative world can be thought of and experienced.

It describes a deep concern of the Jesus movement as it incarnates a new experience of humanity without exclusions and borders. At the heart of Jesus movement were the common people (*ochlos*)—the marginalized and alienated class— who gathered and followed Jesus and enjoyed table fellowship with him (Mark 2:4, 13; 3:9, 20, 32; 4:1; 5:21). Jesus invited them to critique religious institutions and their purity notions that silence, discriminate, and marginalize people in the name of class, gender, race, and sexuality, and thus to "occupy religion."

This *ekklēsia* of the multitude is intrinsic to the meaning of justification by faith, since, for Paul, justification is another word for the reconciliation of Jews and gentiles in Christ and the formation of a new space. Now the *ekklēsia* is this reality that stands squarely in the in-between spaces ('hybrid space'). This 'third space,' to borrow an expression of Homi Bhabha,[37] distinguishes itself from the Jewish

---

[34] Political theorists Michael Hardt and Antonio Negri popularized the term "multitude." See *Empire* (Cambridge, Massachusetts: Harvard University Press, 2000), 60–66, 73–74, 90, 164, 353; idem, *Multitude: War and Democracy in the Age of Empire* (New York: Penguin, 2004), 97–227.

[35] The term "multitude" can be translated as "*minjung.*" A new interpretation of *ochlos* ("crowd") in the Bible stimulated South Korean theologians to develop what is known as *minjung* theology in the 1970's during their struggle against the dictatorial Park Chung-Hee government. *Minjung* reminds of the notion of class, which is now promoted by the Occupy movement.

[36] Hardt and Negri, *Multitude*, 355.

[37] Homi Bhabha, *The Location of Culture* (New York: Routledge, 1994), 36–39.

and gentile territories not as demarcated territory but as something that could be called anti-territorial. In the case of 'the third space' called the *ekklēsia*, the first challenge is not be hospitable to the gentiles ('other') but to be in their place as guest, accepting the terms of the other. In the words of Giorgio Agamben, it means "exiling oneself to the other as he or she is."[38]

While Paul carefully links justification by faith to Abrahamic traditions, he also closely connects justification to baptismal traditions (1 Cor 1:30; 6:11; 2 Cor 1:21–22; Rom 3:25; 4:25; 6:3–4).[39] In doing so, Paul makes the *ekklēsia* a more inclusive, egalitarian and democratic space. But, it does not form spontaneously. Through baptism both Jews and gentiles are united, and therefore must relate to one another differently as part of 'one body.' The image of 'one organic body' was originally used by the Roman empire to justify organic hierarchy; there is no shifting of roles or positions in organic hierarchy. The feet can never dream of becoming the head and vice versa, but head and feet need each other.

The caste system in India also operates on the same Roman imperial logic of organic hierarchy and 'fixity' of identity. It simultaneously manifests two tendencies: one, segmental and other, organic. As a segmental reality, each caste or a sub-caste tends to articulate mutual repulsion, social distance and social inequality, but as an organic system, the caste segments are mutually interlinked by a principle of reciprocity through the *jajmani* system.[40] The caste stratification is a 'closed organic stratification' in contra-distinction with the class principle which is based on 'segmentary stratification.'

---

[38] Giorgio Agamben, *The Coming Community* (trans., Michael Hardt; Minneapolis: University of Minnesota Press, 2007), 23.

[39] Schnelle, *Apostle Paul*, 300.

[40] Etymologically, the term *Jajman* has been derived from the Sanskrit word *Yajman*, which means a person who performs a *yajna*. Thus if some yajna is to be performed for that the services of some Brahmins are essentially needed. It was gradually that its use was made common to everyone who hired services or to whom the services were given. It could be said that the *Jajmani* system is a system of distribution whereby high caste land owning families are provided services and products of various lower castes such as *Khati* (Carpenter), *Nai* (Barber), *Kumhars* (Potters), *Lohars* (Blacksmiths), *Dhobi* (Washer man), *Chuhra* (Sweeper) etc.

Paul, however, turns this organically hierarchical image of the body and 'fixity' of essence upside down, and envisages a more relational and nonhierarchical paradigm:

> "The eye cannot say to the hand, "I have no need of you," nor again the head to the feet, "I have no need of you." On the contrary, the parts of the body which seem to be weaker are indispensable, and those parts of the body which we think less honorable we invest with the greater honor, and our unpresentable parts are treated with greater modesty, which our more presentable parts do not require....If one member suffers, all suffer together; if one member is honored, all rejoice together (1Cor 12:21–26 RSV).

In this respect, the body of Christ (*ekklēsia*) models the multitude. Such a multitude, as Hardt and Negri rightly points out, does not happen automatically but through "the articulations on the plane of immanence without hegemony"[41] and through "the conflictual and cooperative interactions of singularities in the common."[42] Therefore we agree with Hardt and Negri that the debate needs to shift from *being* the multitude to *making* the multitude. The *ekklēsia* of multitude clearly rejects the complacency and sufficiency of the *ekklēsia* itself. In short, the *ekklēsia* of the multitude that justification by faith in Pauline theology envisages is an *ekklēsia* beyond (or without) walls, *for* and *by* the multitude, nurtured by a *habitus* of resistance, contextual in nature, subverts hierarchical power dynamics, and disrupts societal common sense.

Conclusion

Reformation is not primarily a movement against clericalism and mystification of church and its doctrines. There is more to it. If so, justification by faith is not basically a soteriological or doctrinal issue, but a socio-political "occupy movement" of the multitude which (1)

---

41 Michael Hardt and Antonio Negri, *Commonwealth* (Cambridge, Massachusetts: The Belknap Press of Harvard University Press, 2011), 171

42 Hardt and Negri, *Commonwealth*, 175.

critiques religious institutions that monopolize salvation, and silence the marginalized, (2) envisions a democratic and inclusive church, and a secular state, (3) transforms narrow notions of nationalism and patriotism, (4) demystifies church doctrines that justifies social inequality, (5) interrogates the boundaries between sacred and profane, and (6) redefines transcendence not as opposed to immanence, but as an alternative form of immanence that challenges the immanence of the status quo and hierarchy. Therefore, Reformation is not, and it cannot be, a closed movement or an event because it is about humanity first, church second. Reformation will continue so far as humanity bears the image of God which is democratic, inclusive, and non-hierarchical secular in nature.

Chapter 7

Luther, Scripture, and Resistance

"Here I stand, I can do no other, so help me God. Amen"
(Martin Luther)

Introduction

The term 'Reformation' (from Latin *reformatio*, literally 'restoration, renewal') is used in a number of senses: Lutheranism, the Reformed Church (often referred to as 'Calvinism'), the 'Radical Reformation' (often still referred to as 'Anabaptism'), and the 'Counter-Reformation' or 'Catholic Reformation'. In its broadest sense, therefore, the term 'Reformation' is used to refer to all four movements. The term is also used in a somewhat restricted sense to mean 'the magisterial Reformation' or 'mainstream Reformation,'[1]

[1] The 'magisterial Reformation' draws attention to the manner in which the mainstream reformers related to secular authorities—princes, magistrates or city councils. Whereas the radical reformers regarded such authorities as having no rights within the church, the mainstream reformers argued that the church was, at least to some extent, subject to secular authority. The term 'magisterial Reformation' indicated the close connection between the magistracy and the church, which lay at the heart of the reforming programme of Luther.

thereby excluding the Catholic Reformation. In this sense, it refers to the three Protestant movements mentioned above.[2] Therefore, as Alister McGrath rightly contends, it is more accurate to speak of Protestantisms, in the Plural.[3] However, in many scholarly works, the term 'Reformation' is used to refer to that linked with the Lutheran and Reformed churches, and excluding the Anabaptists.[4]

The idea of '*sola scriptura*' (Latin: 'by scripture alone') is regarded as one of the greatest slogans of the reformers, Luther in particular, as they sought to reform the practices and beliefs of the church. If *sola fide* was the 'material principle' of the so-called Protestant Reformation, the principle of *sola scriptura* was its 'formal principle.'[5] If the reformers dethroned the papal supremacy, they enthroned scripture. Every strand of the Reformation regarded scripture as the quarry from which its ideas and practices were hewn.

But, *sola scriptura* was more than a mere enthronement of scripture. The ekklēsial authorities, especially pope, used the scripture so as to validate his supremacy, to reinforce clericalism

---

[2] The term 'Protestant' also requires comment. It derives from the aftermath of the Second Diet of Speyer (February 1529), which voted to end the toleration of Lutheranism in Germany. In April of the same year, six German princes and fourteen cities protested against this oppressive measure, defending freedom of conscience and the rights of religious minorities. The term 'Protestant' derives from this protest. It is therefore not strictly correct to apply the term 'Protestant' to individuals prior to April 1529 or to speak of events prior to that date as constituting 'the Protestant Reformation.' The term 'evangelical' is often used in the literature to refer to the reforming factions at Wittenberg and elsewhere (e.g. in France and Switzerland) prior to this date. Although the word 'Protestant' is often used to refer to this earlier period, this use is, strictly speaking, an anachronism.

[3] Alister McGrath, *Christianity's Dangerous Idea: The Protestant Revolution––A History from the Sixteenth Century to the Twenty-First* (New York: Harper One, 2007), 62–63.

[4] In this paper, unless specified otherwise, I use the term 'Reformation' in the sense of 'Lutheran Reformation.'

[5] 'Formal principle' and 'material principle' are two categories in christian theology to identify and distinguish the authoritative source of theology (formal principle) from the theology itself, especially the central doctrine of that theology (material principle), of a religion, religious movement, tradition, body, denomination, or organization. A 'formal principle' tends to be texts or revered leaders of the religion, while a 'material principle' is its central teaching.

and to silence the laity. The scripture was in Roman vernacular (Latin) and not available for the ordinary members of the church for reading and interpretation. Therefore, Luther re-defines the medieval understanding of scripture to fight against papal hegemony and clerical infallibility. This paper attempts to examine how and how Luther used his view of the scripture as a tool for his resistance movement against papacy and clericalism.

Medieval Christendom and the Roman Catholic View of Scripture

In his treatise, *To the Christian Nobility of the German Nation*, Luther shows how the papal see and Romanists have very cleverly built three walls around themselves to buttress and to protect its supremacy, absolutism, power, and infallibility: popes have made decrees and declared that the spiritual power is above the temporal; only popes may interpret the scriptures; and, no one may summon a council but the pope.[6] However, the papal see has successfully achieved and maintained supremacy primarily by its characteristic view of the scripture in the following ways:

1. The Doctrine of the Infallibility and Inerrancy of the Scripture: The Roman popes enforced the doctrine of the infallibility and inerrancy of the Holy Scripture. According to the Roman church, it is far from being possible that any error can co-exist with inspiration, that inspiration not only is essentially incompatible with error, but excludes and rejects it. It is impossible that God can utter that which is not true. And such an affirmation of scriptural infallibility and inerrancy apparently secures for papal see no greater degree of unanimity when the meaning of the Bible is being interpreted.
2. Biblical Criticism as Disparagement of the Bible: Infallibility and inerrancy was the form in which the Roman church represents and maintains the authority of the scripture. It therefore found it

[6] Martin Luther, *To the Christian Nobility of the German Nation, LW 44* (translated by Charles M. Jacobs; revised by James Atkinson), in Martin Luther, *Three Treatises* (2nd rev edn.; Philadelphia: Fortress, 1970), 1–113, here 11.

necessary to condemn biblical criticism as a deliberate vilification of the Bible.

3. Divinization of Latin Language: Even though a number of vernacular versions of scripture such as Wycliffite translation,[7] in spite of them being direct translations of the Vulgate (*textus vulgutus* or "the common text"), the medieval church condemned this process of translation. The church condemned not only translation but also their use by the clergy and the laity as such initiatives posed implicit challenge to the teaching authority of the church. Moreover, the Latin-reading elite deprived the ordinary christians from reading the scripture.[8] This enabled the Roman church to stop the rank and file from the critical study of the scriptures and the general practice of Bible reading: "The church cannot be for 'the open Bible' at any price."[9]
4. Obscurity and Ambiguity of the Scripture: The medieval church taught its members that it is impossible for the average christians to unveil the meaning hidden in the scripture as it is obscure. Most of the members were not familiar with Latin either. Nevertheless the church did not accept the translations into the vernacular because obscurity of the scripture was regarded as an intrinsic part of 'scripturality.'
5. Knowledge of the Scripture as an Ontological Endowment: The medieval church hierarchy believed that some 'secret knowledge' must be lodged somewhere in the church, especially in the clergy. It means that clergy possess a 'special knowledge' that is kept 'secret' from most baptized members, a knowledge not

[7] John Wycliffe was an English scholastic philosopher, theologian, Biblical translator, reformer, and seminary professor at Oxford. He was an influential dissident within the Roman Catholic priesthood during the 14th century. Wycliffe attacked the privileged status of the clergy, which was central to their powerful role in England. He then attacked the luxury and pomp of local parishes and their ceremonies. Wycliffe was also an advocate for translation of the Bible into the vernacular. He completed a translation directly from the Vulgate into Middle English in the year 1382, now known as Wycliffe's Bible.

[8] N. T. Wright, *Scripture and the Authority of God: How to Read the Bible Today* (New York: Harper One, 2011), 73.

[9] C. J. Cadoux, *Catholicism and Christianity*, (London: George Allen & Unwin, 1928), 267 n.10.

shared by all believers; clergy is 'ontologically endowed' with the gift of interpretation to be dispensed at will. Consequently, the Apostolic See of Rome controlled the evangelic rhetoric and the interpretation of the scripture.

6. The Church as the Sole Legitimate and Infallible Interpreter of the Scripture: Interpretation is the *proprium* of the whole church. But, the Roman church has construed it in a different sense. This sense is exemplified by the restrictions it imposed upon the use of scriptures by the ordinary members. More importantly, the church as the sole interpreter holds the pope to be the ultimate interpreter, and under him the Roman clerical hierarchy in their order, each rank having its appropriate degree of authority.
   Behind this understanding of the church as the sole interpreter,[10] there are many considerations and affirmations: the church is the owner of the scripture; scripture is the statement of the teaching the church; the church is the living voice of Christ; the Bible by itself is wrapped in a certain religious obscurity; and, any principle of interpretation other than the Roman church leads immediately to a chaos of individualism.
7. Identification of Scripture and Doctrine: The church possesses the living voice of Christ. Therefore, scripture can say, and by interpretation can be made to say, nothing that conflicts with the ecclesiastical doctrine. Thus, the Roman church established the identification of scripture and doctrine. In other words, scriptural interpretation is made subject to dogma. The church thus controls and channels the scripture.
8. Authority of the Scripture: For Roman church, authority of the scripture is not intrinsic but external and derivative; the scripture draws the vigour and the authority from the church. Thus is introduced one of the cardinal arguments for subordinating scripture to the church; the church is prior to the scripture, and hence superior to the scripture.

All these facts throw disquieting light upon Roman practice and action with respect to the Holy Scripture.

---

[10] Luther, *To the Christian Nobility of the German Nation,* 18–20.

The Cry for Reform: The Socio-religious Backdrop to the Reformation

The background of Luther Reformation is medieval period. Therefore, one must locate the Lutheran movement against the intellectual and political forces in the medieval Europe that either triggered or necessitated it.

Lorenzo Valla's Refutation in 1440: The 'unholy' nexus between religion and state was sustained for centuries by the "Donation of Constantine" (*Donatio Constantini and Constitutum Constantini*),[11] the document purporting to record the Roman emperor Constantine's bestowal of vast territory and spiritual and temporal power on Pope Sylvester I (reigned 314–335) and his successors.[12] Leo IX (1049–54) was the first pope to cite it as an authority in an official act, and subsequent popes used it in their struggles with the Roman emperors and other secular leaders. Various ecclesiastics included it in their codes of canon law, and even Rome's opponents seldom questioned its authenticity.

The Donation had great influence on the political and religious life in medieval Europe, until it was clearly demonstrated to be a forgery by the famous Italian humanist Lorenzo Valla. In 1440 Lorenzo Valla showed that the Latin used in the document was not that of the 4th century. At the dawn of Reformation, Luther had read Valla's repudiation and convinced other reformers that the document was the forgery of the Antichrist embodied by the one

---

[11] Martin Luther, *To the Christian Nobility of the German Nation*, 54–55.

[12] The Donation was based on the Legenda S. Silvestri (Latin: "The Legend of St. Sylvester"), a 5th-century account of the relationship between Pope Sylvester I and the emperor Constantine. It begins with the tale of the conversion of Constantine to Christianity after Sylvester I miraculously cured him of leprosy. Constantine then declares the importance of Rome to the church because it is the city of the apostles Peter and Paul. The second section of the forgery contains the actual donation: Constantine, in preparing to depart to his new capital of Constantinople, bestows upon the pope supremacy over the sees of Antioch, Alexandria, Constantinople, and Jerusalem and all the world's churches. He next grants administrative rights to Sylvester and his successors over estates granted to churches throughout the empire. Most importantly, Constantine gives the pope control of the imperial palace in Rome and all the regions of the Western Empire; this effectively conveys the notion that the pope has the right to appoint secular rulers in the West.

seated on the papal throne.[13] This caused an unprecedented revolt against European clericalism, Papal tyranny and Roman Catholic magisterium.

1. The Great Schism: The authority of the pope was called into question through the Great Schism or Papal Schism (1378–1417) and its aftermath. The Great Schism was a split within the Catholic church concerning the authority of pope as there were two rival claimants to papacy—Urban VI and Clement VII, who led the Italian and the French factions respectively. This situation continued until 1417, when the council of Constance elected Martin V as pope. For a brief period around 1409, there were three claimants to papacy.
   The crucial questions were: how could the dispute concerning who was *really* the pope be resolved; and, *which* pope should settle the doctrinal disputes? Eventually the Council of Constance was convened (1414–1417) to settle the authority dispute. There were two rival theories/factions of authority with in the church: those who held that the supreme doctrinal authority resided in a General Council ('conciliarist' position), and those who argued that it resided in the person of the pope ('curialist' postion). As a result, it seemed that an important general principle had been established: councils have authority over pope. The victory of the 'conciliarist' faction over the 'curialist' faction eventually posed a challenge to the doctrinal authority of the pope.
2. The Rise of 'Secular' Rulers: The rise in the power of 'secular' rulers of Europe, who increasingly came to regard the pope's propels as somewhat irrelevant. Nationalism became an increasingly important factor in reducing the authority of pope and increasing the power of secular European governments. Anti-papal feeling increased in Germany because papacy was often linked to Italy. In 1478 the Spanish Inquisition was established, with power over clergy and religious orders (and eventually over bishops)—and the control of this system of courts rested not with the pope, but with the Spanish king. The dramatic

[13] Heiko Oberman, *Luther: Man between God and the Evil* (New York: Image, 1992), 42.

victory of Francis I over the combined papal and Swiss force in 1515 established his authority over the French church. The ensuing Concordat of Bologna (1516) gave Francis I the right to appoint all the senior clergy, which in turn weakened the direct papal authority over that church. More importantly, Francis I, delegated responsibility of enforcing religious orthodoxy to the Faculty of Theology of the University of Paris.

A further illustration of the severe restrictions placed upon papal authority by secular forces can be seen in the case of Henry VIII's attempt to divorce Catherine of Aragon. At the time when Henry petitioned pope for a divorce (which would normally have been forthcoming without undue difficulty), the pope found himself under tremendous pressure from emperor Charles V—who had been related to Catherine. As Charles had recently attacked Rome and retained a large military presence in that region, the pope was faced with the choice of offending either the king (who had no army anywhere near Rome) or the emperor. The outcome was a forgone conclusion: Henry VIII did not get a divorce. There was thus a twofold crisis of authority in the medieval church: *theological* authority; and, *political* authority.

3. The Rise in Anti-clericalism: There were many factors that contributed to the phenomenon of anti-clericalism: the poor quality of the rank and file clergy; and, the exemption of the clergy from taxation, prosecution in civil courts, and compulsory military service.[14] This not only provoked popular irritation, anti-clerical attitude, and considerable local resentment, especially in the times of economic difficulty (e.g. subsistence crisis in France in 1520), but also widened the distance between the clergy and the working class. The somewhat mandatory noble background of the bishops and the clergy served to distance them from the artisans and peasants. Hostility to the clergy was greatest among the ordinary people who resented

[14] The best study is Hans-Jurgen Goertz, *Pfaffenhass und gross Geschrei: Die reformatorischen Bewegungen in Deutschland 1517-1529* (Munich: C. H. Beck, 1987); see also H. J. Cohn, "Anti-clericalism in the German Peasants" War, 1525," *Past and Present* 83 (1979), 3–31.

their privilege and the oppressive role often played by the clergy as the landlords to the German peasants.

4. Erasmus of Rotterdam: If any figure stands head and shoulder above other northern European humanists, not least in terms of his influence upon German Reformation, it was the Dutch Renaissance humanist Desiderius Erasmus Roterodamus, known as Erasmus or Erasmus of Rotterdam.[15] The most important humanist work to circulate in Europe during the first decades of the 16th century was Erasmus' *Enchiridion militis Christiani* ('Handbook of the Christian Soldier').[16] A number of features of this book are of decisive importance for Lutheran reformation:

    i. The revolutionary character of Erasmus' *Enchiridion* lies in its daring new suggestion that the strengthening of the laity holds the key to witness revival of the church. He questioned the notion of clergy's permanent superiority over the laity. Therefore, the scripture must be made available to all.
    ii. Erasmus' strong emphasis on inner religiosity results in an understanding of christianity which makes no reference to the church—its rites, priests and institutions.

Erasmus realized that the anti-papal and anti-clerical movement will be successful only if their monopoly over the scripture, Roman understanding of the inerrancy and infallibility of the scripture, and the divinization of the Latin language are challenged. His discovery in 1505 of the Lorenzo Valla's 15th century notes on the Greek text of the New Testament accentuated the movement. Drawing on Lorenzo Valla's works

[15] For the full extent of humanist influence upon the reformer, see Alister McGrath, *The Intellectual Origins of the European Reformation* (Oxford: Blackwell, 1987), 122–39, 152–74.

[16] The word '*enchiridion*' literally means 'something held in the hand.' And came to have two meanings: a 'weapon' held in the hand (e.g. dagger) or a book held in the hand (e.g. 'handbook'). See Erika Rummel, "The Theology of Erasmus," in *The Cambridge Companion to Reformation Theology* (eds., David Bagchi, and David C. Steinmetz; Cambridge: Cambridge University Press, 2004), 28–38.

and his textual techniques capable of establishing accurately the best text of scripture, Erasmus published Greek New Testament (*Novum Instrumentum omne*) in 1516. Erasmus showed that a Vulgate translation of a number of NT texts could not be justified. There was thus a general loss of confidence in the inerrancy and infallibility of the Vulgate, which medieval church used to validate its beliefs and practices.[17] No longer could 'scripture' and 'the Vulgate text' be regarded as one and the same thing. Erasmus' new translation of the Greek NT seemed to many to call the papalism into question. For the reformers, however, these developments were nothing less than providential.

5. The Rise of 'Doctrinal Pluralism' (Polydoxy?): One of the most significant features of medieval religious thought was the emergence of various 'schools' of theology. The expansion of universities and schools facilitated the expansion of intellectual diversification.[18] It is important to recognize that the schools differed in their understandings on a number of major doctrinal issues. Moreover, as Edward Schillebeekx correctly observes, "a marked difference arose between the *magisterium episcoporum* and the *magisterium theologorum*, a field of tension which has led to much crossing of boundaries on both sides" because unlike the magisters or doctors in theology from universities, the bishops had hardly enough theological training.[19] As a result the papacy was reluctant to define, and apparently incapable of enforcing, 'true dogma.' It raised a few issues: which corresponds most closely to the teaching of the scripture; and, what was the teaching of the church? This set the stage for a 'doctrinal pluralism.'

---

[17] R. Loewe, "The Medieval History of the Latin Vulgate," in *Cambridge Dictionary of the Bible II: The West from the Fathers to the Reformation* (ed., G. W. H. Lampe; Cambridge: Cambridge University Press, 1969), 102–54.

[18] On the origins and impact of doctrinal pluralism, see McGrath, *The Intellectual Origins of the European Reformation*, 12–28.

[19] Edward Schillebeekx, *Church: The Human Story of God* (New York: Crossroad, 1994), 225.

'*Sola Scriptura*' and the Lutheran Resistance Movement

The doctrine/principle of *sola scriptura* is not an invention of the Lutheran Reformation. Many Pre-Reformation thinkers, like John Wycliffe (1320–1384) and John Huss (1372–1415), used this principle and placed higher emphasis on the authority of scripture than was expressed at the Council of Trent by the Roman Catholic church; Luther inherited *sola scriptura* from medieval theologians and philosophers. The Pre-Reformers used *sola scriptura* mainly to deal with the events unleashed by European Enlightenment, especially the rise of biblical criticism.

There were two options left for those who felt the impact of critical rationality and wanted to remain faithful to the scripture: fundamentalism and foundationalism. While fundamentalism means to surrender 'reason' and cling to the literal sense of the scripture (*sacrificium intellectus*), foundationalism means to ground faith on some foundation other than scripture such as moral postulates or a ground of being or revelation. Fundamentalism opted for the truths of history without the use of 'reason', whereas foundationalism sought the truth of 'reason' without historical claims of the scripture.

But the *sola scriptura* principle for the reformers addressed not historicity or reason or logic but power relations: who and what controls the authority of the scripture and its interpretations? Therefore, reformation thinkers, especially Luther, used *sola scriptura* to oppose the absolute claims of papalism and clericalism, and the hierarchical power equations associated with it. This Luther effectively achieved in many ways:

1. Authority of the Scripture: Contrary to the Catholic view, Luther argued that the authority of the scripture is intrinsic; scripture derives its authority from itself. Thus Luther loosed the idea of the authority of the scripture from the authority of the pope and ekklēsial institutions. In other words, the dispute between Luther and Rome lies not in the authority of the scripture, but in the question where does the scripture derive its authority from.
   Clarity of the scripture (often called 'the Perspicuity of Scripture'): The Roman church emphasized the ambiguity and

obscurity of the scripture to reinforce clericalism and papal absolutism: "on this account I have attacked the pope, in whose kingdom nothing is more commonly stated or more generally accepted than the idea that the scriptures are obscure and ambiguous, so that the spirit to interpret them must be sought from the Apostolic see of Rome."[20] But, Luther advocated the clearness of scripture (*claritas scripturae*) in one his best works/ treatises, "*On the Bondage of the Will*" (1529): "The Scriptures are perfectly clear."[21] The solemn Protestation of the Diet of Speyer (1529) also sets out the Reformation position: "This Holy Book is in all things necessary for the Christian; it shines clearly in its own light."[22] This explains why Luther speaks of *sola scriptura* as 'formal principle' and *sola gratia* as the 'material principle.'[23]

However, scripture's clarity does not mean that reading works *ex opere operato*, as if simply pronouncing the words magically yields the meaning. Nor does Luther sound fundamentalist in his claim that the scripture is not obscure.[24] For Luther, obscurity of the scripture is the result of human resistance: "It is true that for many people much remains abstruse; but this is not due to the obscurity of scripture, but the blindness or indolence of those

---

[20] Martin Luther, *Luther's Works,* vol. 33: *Career of the Reformer III* (ed., Jaroslav Pelikan and Helmut Lehman; Philadelphia: Fortress, 1972), 33:90.

[21] Luther, *Luther's Works,* 33:99.

[22] Cited in Timothy George, *Reading Scripture with the Reformers* (Downers Grove, IL: IVP Academic, 2011), 119.

[23] August Twesten, *Vorlesungen Über Die Dogmatik Der Evangelisch-Lutherischen Kirche, Nach Dem Compendium Des Herrn W. M. L. De Wette* (2nd ed.; Hamburg: Friedrich, 1929), 280–82. See the informative essay by Erik M. Heen, "The Distinction 'Material/Formal principles' and Its Use in American Lutheran Theology," LQ 17/3 (Autumn 2003), 329–54.

[24] Miikka Ruokanen, *Doctrina Divinitus Inspirata: Martin Luther's Position in the Ecumenical problem of Biblical Inspiration* (Helsinki: Vammala, 1985), 146: "Luther's principle of *theologia crucis* legitimates the critical approach to the Bible avoiding all divinization of the letter.... But...applying an external criterion to the theological evaluation of the Bible would mean applying ideological criticism alien to the essence of the Christian faith."

who will not take the trouble to look at the very clearest truth."[25] It means that those whose eyes of the heart (Eph 1:18) have been opened by the Spirit cannot miss the main story.
In other words, as Francis Turretin argues, "The Scriptures are so plain in things essential to salvation…that without the external aid of tradition or the infallible judgment of the church, they may be read and understood profitably by believers."[26] Therefore, for Luther, the perceived obscurity of the scripture does not call for a 'secret knowledge' nor for an intrinsic (and ontological) endowment given to the pope and the clergy to be dispensed at will, but necessitates prayer and meditation. Thus Luther challenges papalism and clericalism.

2. "Scripture Interprets Itself (*scriptura sui ipsius interpres*):" Luther's often-quoted slogan "scripture interprets itself,"[27] which literally means "the scripture is in itself the interpreter:" It implies that scripture cannot be taken captive by the papal see. This principle is useful for texts that are "hard to understand" (2 Pet 3:16). In such cases the part interprets the whole and the whole interprets the part. The reformers insisted that clearer portions of scripture illumine passages that are less clear. The deficiency is not with the scripture but with our limited knowledge of its vocabulary and context.[28] To put it simply: it is not the church that interprets scripture but the scripture that interprets the church.
3. The Priesthood of all Believers: In his *Address to the Christian Nobility* (1520), Luther coupled *sola scriptura* and priesthood of all. Luther maintained that the right to read and interpret the scripture is not the exclusive ontological prerogative of the clergy and the pope, but the fundamental right of all members of the faith community on the basis of the spiritual priesthood

---

[25] Luther, *Luther's Works*, 33:27.

[26] Francis Turretin, *Institutes of Elenctic Theology*, vol.1, *First through Tenth Topics*, trans. George Musgrave Giger (ed. James T. Dennison Jr.; Phillipsburg, NJ: P&R, 1992), 2.17.7.

[27] Martin Luther, *D. Martin Luthers Werke: Kritische Gesamtausgabe* (Weimar: Böhlau, 1883–2009), 7:97.19–24.

[28] See further Mark D. Thompson, *A Clear and Present Word: The Clarity of Scripture* (Downers Grove, IL: InterVarsity, 2006).

shared by all believers. Against the absolutist claims of the 'Romanist', as he called the papal hierarchy and its clergy, that they alone constituted the spiritual estate (*geistlich stand*), Luther interpreted several passages (1 Peter 2:9; 1 Cor 12:12–13; Rev 5:9–10) to mean that all those have "one baptism, one gospel, one faith…are all Christians alike; for baptism, gospel, and faith alone make us spiritual and Christian people;"[29]

For Luther, "we are all consecrated priests through baptism."[30] That means, Luther continues, "when a bishop consecrates it is nothing else than that…he takes a person and charges him to exercise this power on behalf of the others."[31] Therefore, "a priest in Christendom is nothing else but an officeholder."[32] It follows from this argument that "there is no true, basic difference between laymen and priests…except for the sake of office and work [*den des ampts odder wercks halben*], but not for the sake of status [*stand*]."[33] In other words, Luther insisted that the distinction between priests and laity is functional, not ontological.

Consequently, argued Luther, all christians "have the power to test and judge what is right or wrong in matters of faith." Luther took a verse that had usually been applied to the pope (1 Cor 2:15: "A spiritual man judges all things and is judged by no one") and applied it to all christians, since they were the spiritual people entitled to render judgment.[34] Therefore, the "claim that only the pope may interpret the scripture is an outrageous fancied fable."[35]

With this model, Luther disputed the claims of the Roman papal hierarchy on the basis of *sola scripture* while at the same time he tried to avoid the arbitrariness of individual becoming the final authority and the resultant 'hermeneutical havoc.' His translation of the NT into the vernacular initiated the process of making the

---

[29] Luther, *To the Christian Nobility of the German Nation,* 12.

[30] Luther, *To the Christian Nobility of the German Nation,* 12.

[31] Luther, *To the Christian Nobility of the German Nation,* 12.

[32] Luther, *To the Christian Nobility of the German Nation,* 14.

[33] Luther, *To the Christian Nobility of the German Nation,* 14.

[34] Luther, *To the Christian Nobility of the German Nation,* 21.

[35] Luther, *To the Christian Nobility of the German Nation,* 20.

scripture more accessible to all believers and enabled them to exercize the power to interpret it to which their decentralized and democratic priesthood entitled them. Thus, Luther democratized not only the *ekklēsia* but the scripture itself.

Scripture, Power, and Reformation

The Roman Catholic church used the scripture as a papal text to consolidate papal power, clericalism and hierarchical hegemony. As an ekklēsial text, therefore, scripture functioned as a hegemonic institution to legitimize the absolute doctrinal power of popes and perpetuate their economic and political interests by subjugating and silencing the voice of the laity and the so-called ordinary members of the *ekklēsia*. This they achieved somewhat primarily through their strategic production of ekklēsial/doctrinal knowledge concerning the scripture.

According to Edward Said, the key to any form of power is knowledge, and true power is held with the conviction that the ruler knows better than the ruled, and must convince the ruled that whatever the ruler does is for the benefit of the ruled. What was strikingly different about Said's work was that he was able to establish the intimate connection between production of knowledge and power. The assumption undergirding this thinking is the belief that "knowledge of the subject [ruled]…is what makes their management easy and profitable; knowledge gives power, more power requires more knowledge, and so on in an increasingly profitable dialectic of information and control."[36] In other words, knowledge is made possible by power, and power is effective because of knowledge.

Prior to the Reformation, the papal see regulated all the production of scriptural knowledge and excluded possible competing scriptural discourses. To monopolize the production of scriptural knowledge and condemn/exclude other discourses, they designed various doctrines and insisted various theological assumptions concerning the authority of the scripture. For the Roman church, the

[36] Edward Said, *Orientalism* (London: Penguin, 1985), 36. Said is indebted to Michael Foucault for the connection between knowledge and power. See Michel Foucault, *Discipline and Punish. The Birth of the Prison* (Middlesex: Penguin Books, 1982).

authority of the scripture is not intrinsic but attributed by the church as the latter is chronologically prior to the former. Moreover, it is the church that possesses the living voice of Christ. Scripture does not say anything that contradicts the doctrines of the church; they equated scripture with the doctrines of the church. In this respect, the scripture is infallible and inerrant. In other words, the authority of the scripture is subject to the authority of the papal see. Therefore, if any one questions the authority of the pope using the scripture is in effect questioning the authority of the scripture itself.

To legitimize the papal authority further, the Roman church effectively used the doctrine of infallibility and inerrancy of the scripture to exclude and disparage other competing discourses such as biblical criticism. In order to stop the laity from reading and interpreting the scripture, the Roman church discouraged its printing and translation into the vernacular. They also insisted that only the clergy and the pope who have the ontologically endowed 'secret knowledge' can interpret the scripture because of its inherent ambiguity and obscurity. As a result, the production of scriptural knowledge by the laity is made perpetually irrational and illogical. And the papal see used its institutional apparatus to act as 'normalizing judges' and regard or verify the epistemic discourses of the laity. The church maintained such an epistemic division between the true knowledge of the clergy and the false knowledge of the laity to keep the authority of the church to interpret the scripture intact. This disciplinary power is "calculated, organized and technically thought out."[37]

However, the Saidian discourse analysis is operated on the notion of a binary between the ruler and the ruled.[38] A few postcolonial critics like Homi Bhabha[39] and Gayatri Spivak[40] disapprove such a binary discourse. They argue that there is no overly

[37] Foucault, *Discipline and Punish*, 26–29.

[38] Said tends to transcend the notion of binary and appreciate cultural hybridity later: see *Culture and Imperialism* (London: Vintage, 1994), 1–72.

[39] Homi Bhabha, *The Location of Culture* (London/New York: Routledge, 1995).

[40] Gayatri Spivak, *A Critique of Postcolonial Reason: Toward a History of the Vanishing Present* (Calcutta: Seagull Books, 1999).

rigid binary opposition between the ruler and the ruled for both are often caught up in a complex reciprocal relationship of desire and derision. Therefore it is necessary to examine the whole complex of the hybridity or 'in-between' space between the ruler and ruled which can initiate new signs of identity and be innovative sites of collaboration and contestation.[41]

When Foucault discusses power, he does not describe power as idea a fixed, quantitative force or something innately held by individuals or institutions. He acknowledges that power often is channelled through institutions, but this is not due to the 'inherent' power of such people or institutions. Rather, Foucault understands power as force, something present throughout the world and in all people. Power is, therefore, distinct from authority. Everyone has power, whether they exercize individually or through institutions. The interactions between peoples, between people and institutions are not neutral, but "force relations." If so, the interactions between the clergy and the laity in the medieval christendom are power relations.

One reason that initiates change of forces in complex arrangements is resistance. Resistance is an integral part of power, because no arrangement of forces can ever include every force or stop interaction between forces, despite attempts to do so. Resistance may come in the form of outright opposition to a particular arrangement of forces. Because the resistance is outside the dominant arrangement of forces, this resistance will eventually lead to a new arrangement of forces and new exercize of power. Social change is, therefore, always possible.

Foucault also recognized that power is not simply coercive. What makes power appealing, and the reason why people accept particular arrangements of forces, is that power is productive.[42] Power does function in a repressive way in society; Foucault does not deny this aspect of power. But when the power is repressive, people and communities are able to reject such coercion and repression.

---

[41] Spivak, *A Critique of Postcolonial Reason*, 1–2.

[42] Foucault, *Discipline and Punish*, 119.

This better explains the emergence of various resistance movements in the medieval christendom which defy the process of othering by the papal see. The 'in-between' space between the clergy and laity turns out to be the space of resistance. Lorenzo Valla's refutation of the *Donation* caused revolt against clericalism and papacy. The Great Schism initiated the democratization of the church by placing the authority of council over the authority of pope. It also calls into question the nature and scope of the papal authority. Erasmus's production of the Greek New Testament challenged the papal monopoly over the production of scriptural knowledge. The advent of various schools of theology and the expansion of universities not only set the stage for doctrinal pluralism, but created twofold authority in the church–theological and political.

As Foucault correctly argues, the power that institutions exercize is not innate to them, but the result of specific circumstances and historical conditions. Thus, because specific circumstances and conditions made these institutions possible, a change in those circumstances threatens, if not outright negates, the ability of these institutions to continue to exercize their power and to exist in the same way. This explains why and how the various resistance movements thus created "fractures and slippages" in the papal absolutist system. It enabled Luther to initiate a counter discourse concerning the scripture and its interpretation.

Luther must have understood the intimate connection between papalism and knowledge of the scripture. In doing so, he re-imagined and re-defined the very understanding of the scripture itself. First and foremost, he argued that the authority of the scripture is intrinsic; the authority of the scripture is not derived from the authority of the church; the authority church was made subject to the authority of the scripture.

To challenge the whole notion of the church as the custodian of the scripture, Luther translated the Bible into the vernacular. He printed the Bible and made them available to everyone. The availability of the scripture in the vernacular enabled the laity to enter into the production of scripture knowledge. It proved to the laity that the scripture is not as obscure and ambiguous as they were made to believe. No ontological endowment of 'secret knowledge' is required to produce the scriptural knowledge, but the grace of God. According to Luther, it is not the church that interprets scripture but that scripture interprets the church: "scripture interprets itself." It dismantled the ontological distinction between the clergy and the laity.

By inviting and enabling the ordinary laity to participate in the production of scriptural knowledge, Luther democratized the scripture and its interpretation. The papal text now becomes the scripture of the community. The church is no longer the custodian and sole interpreter of the scripture. Consequently, the *ekklēsia* becomes the *ekklēsia* of the multitude. Production of the scriptural knowledge is not ontologically determined but democratically defined. Even the secular schools and universities participate in the knowledge production. In this sense, Luther encouraged the secularization of the production of scripture knowledge.

More importantly, in democratizing the scripture, Luther actually aimed to democratize and decentralize the *ekklēsia*. This Luther achieved primarily by linking *sola scriptura* and the priesthood of all. He outrightly rejected the ontological superiority of the clergy and the myth of their 'secret knowledge.' By demystifying the clergy and the scripture, Luther not only made the clergy a functional arrangement but also de-clericalized the church. Demystification of the scripture leads to the demystification of the church; democratization of the scriptures can make the church democratic and de-clericalized.

Conclusion

Our task of defining the nature of the church is closely connected to how we understand the scripture. Any understanding that holds the scripture as the property of the clergy and the church hierarchy is actually de-democratizing both the scripture and the church. But, one might argue that giving every individual the opportunity to participate in the production of scripture knowledge fits hand in glove with what we may call 'interpretive egoism', 'hermeneutical havoc' and de-sacralization of the scripture. Such a fear is definitely misplaced as it presumes that the church possesses the scripture. On other hand, by democratizing and de-mystifying the scripture, we can make the church a more democratic, decentralized, and dynamic space. Only a de-mystified and democratic church can de-mystify and democratize the scripture and vice versa. Scripture liberates the church, when the church liberates the scripture itself.

Chapter 8

Mind-Body Dualism, and Embodied Anthropology

Introduction

The term 'dualism' (from the Latin word *duo* meaning 'two') denotes the state of two parts. It was originally coined to denote co-eternal binary opposition, a meaning that is preserved in metaphysical and philosophical duality discourses but has been more generalized in other usages to indicate a system which contains two fundamental kinds or categories of things or principles.

'Dualism' has a variety of uses in the history of philosophy and theology. Moral dualism is the belief of the great complement of or conflict between the benevolent and the malevolent. It simply implies that there are two moral opposites at work, independent of any interpretation of what might be 'moral' and independent of how these may be represented. In ontological dualism, the world is divided into two overarching categories.[1] In theology, for example a

[1] The opposition and combination of the universe's two basic principles of *yin* and *yang* is a large part of Chinese philosophy, and is an important feature of

'dualist' is someone who believes that Good and Evil—or God and the Devil[2]—are independent and more or less equal forces in the world.[3] In the philosophy of mind, dualism is the theory that the mental and the physical—or mind and body or mind and brain—are, in some sense, radically different kinds of thing.

In contemporary theology, 'mind-body dualism' is often used to criticize world views which are male chauvinistic (patriarchal), ecologically inimical, and generally disparaging the physical reality/existence. Its historical roots can be traced to both Hebraic and Hellenistic thought forms. Thus, the Biblical accent on divine transcendence and sovereignty is perceived to set God above and beyond the world in a way that undermines our need to connect with one another and to foster relationships of equality and mutual self-giving. Similarly, the Platonic division of mind and body is viewed as leading to the devaluing of the physical world in a way that privileges the mind, denigrates the body and promotes the exploitation of nature/matter.

Mind-Body Dualism: A Historical Trajectory

In 'mind-body dualism', 'mind' is contrasted with 'body', but at different times, different aspects of the mind have been the center of attention. The classical emphasis originates in Plato's *Phaedo*, also known to ancient readers as *On The Soul*, which is one of the best-known dialogues of Plato's middle period, along with the *Republic* and the *Symposium.* The philosophical subject of the dialogue is the immortality of the soul. It is set in the last hours prior to the death

---

Taoism, both as a philosophy and as a religion (it is also discussed in Confucianism).

[2] In theology, *dualism* may refer to duotheism, bitheism, or ditheism. Although ditheism/bitheism imply moral dualism, they are not equivalent: ditheism/bitheism implies (at least) two gods, while moral dualism does not imply any-*theism* (*theo*s=god) whatsoever. Dualism can also refer to the relationship between God and creation, which exists in some traditions of Christianity (e.g. Paulicianism, Catharism, and Gnosticism). The *Dvaita* Vedanta school of Indian philosophy also espouses a dualism between God and the universe.

[3] Dualism contrasts with monism, which is the theory that there is only one fundamental kind, category of thing or principle; and, rather less commonly, with pluralism, which is the view that there are many kinds or categories.

of Socrates, and is Plato's last dialogue to detail the philosopher's final days, following *Euthyphro*, *Apology*, and *Crito*. Plato believed that the true substances are not physical bodies, which are ephemeral, but the eternal 'forms' of which bodies are imperfect copies. As a result, he conceived the material world as evil and "feminine" on the one hand, and the spiritual as good and 'masculine.' This not only succeeded in creating a negative and static dualism between the material and spiritual worlds, but also had a major impact on christian anthropology.

The Platonic understanding of the person as a soul imprisoned in a body created a further disabling dualism between males and females. The association of matter with 'feminity' and evil meant that women were associated more strongly with their bodily natures and the life of the flesh in its fallen state. Men, on the other hand, were deemed to be closer to their higher spiritual nature and the life of the spirit in relation to God. This deeply entrenched association of women with the natural world and evil, and men with the world of spirit. Scholars have traced how later Hebraic and christian thinkers elaborated this Platonic theme in ways which connected it explicitly with the theme of man's rightful domination of both women and nature.[4]

The more modern versions of mind-body dualism have their origin in René Descartes' philosophical treatise *Meditations*, in which the existence of God and the immortality of the soul are demonstrated. Descartes (1596–1650) was a *substance dualist*.[5] There are two important concepts deployed in the notion of 'substance dualism'—*substance* and *dualism*. According to Howard Robinson, "a substance is characterized by its properties, but, according to

---

[4] Genevieve Lloyd, *The Man of Reason: "Male" and "Female" in Western Philosophy* (London: Methuen, 1984), 6. See also Rosemary Radford Ruether, *Sexism and God-Talk: Towards a Feminist Theology* (London: SCM, 1983), 83.

[5] There are two important concepts deployed in this notion. One is that of *substance*, the other is the *dualism* of these substances. A substance is characterized by its properties, but, according to those who believe in substances, it is more than the collection of the properties it possesses, it is *the thing which* possesses them. So the mind is not just a collection of thoughts, but is *that which* thinks, an immaterial substance over and above its immaterial states.

those who believe in substances, it is more than the collection of the properties it possesses, it is *the thing which* possesses them." So the mind is not just a collection of thoughts, but is *that which* thinks, an immaterial substance over and above its immaterial states. This explains why 'substance dualism' is also often called 'Cartesian dualism.'[6] Descartes believed that there were two kinds of substance: 'matter', of which the essential property is that it is spatially extended; and 'mind', of which the essential property is that *it thinks*.

Descartes' conception of the relation between 'mind' and 'body' was quite different from that held in the Aristotelian tradition. For Aristotle, there is no exact science of matter. How matter behaves is essentially affected by the form that is in it. You cannot combine just any matter with any form—you cannot make a knife out of butter, nor a human being out of paper—so the nature of the matter is a necessary condition for the nature of the substance. But, the nature of the substance does not follow from the nature of its matter alone: there is no 'bottom up' account of substances. Matter is a determinable made determinate by form. This was how Aristotle explained the connection of soul to body: a particular soul exists as the organizing principle in a particular parcel of matter.

The crux of Descartes' method is radical doubt. He doubts everything he can manage to doubt—all traditional knowledge, the impressions of his senses, and even the fact that he has a body—until he reaches one thing he cannot doubt, the existence of himself as a thinker. Thus, he arrives at his celebrated philosophical proposition, *Cogito, ergo sum* ("I think, therefore I exist"), originally appeared in his *Discourse on the Method.* This proposition became a fundamental element of Western philosophy, as it claimed to form a secure foundation for knowledge in the face of radical doubt. From this Descartes deduces that the essence of human nature lies in thought, and that all the things we conceive clearly and distinctly are true.

---

[6] But some substance dualists like Lowe is keen to distinguish their theories from Descartes's. See Edward Jonathan Lowe, "Non-Cartesian substance dualism and the problem of mental causation," *Erkenntnis*, 65/1 (2006), 5–23.

Descartes' *cogito,* as it has come to be called, made 'mind' more certain for him than 'matter' and led him to the conclusion that the two were separate and fundamentally different. Thus, he asserted that there is nothing included in the concept of 'body' that belongs to the 'mind;' and nothing in that of 'mind' that belongs to the 'body'. The Cartesian division between 'mind' and 'matter' has had a profound effect on Western thought. It has taught us to be aware of ourselves as isolated egos existing "inside" our bodies. Descartes based his whole view of nature on this fundamental division between two independent and separate realms; that of mind, or *res cogitans,* the 'thinking thing', and that of matter, or *res extensa,* the 'extended thing'. In other words, 'mind' is a substance completely distinct from the 'body.' Thereafter human reason became the sole key to unlocking the external world, with nature becoming a vast soulless plane of matter to be examined, ordered, and classified by the human mind.

Artificial Intelligence (AI): The New Dualism/Cartesianism?

The computer model of the mind, pioneered by Alan Turing's strong Artificial Intelligence (AI) thesis prophesied the development of software that would enable computers to stimulate human 'intelligence.'[7] The potential that human have to create a machine that may successfully stimulate human capacities is at once attractive and threatening. However, to create a machine in the human image (capacity to reason) is not equivalent to creating a person. There are differences between the ways in which the brain and the computer process information although many in the AI community dispute this observation. It is a question of whether a dynamic system such as the nervous system can be modelled by a computer, after all the brain is not a computer and consciousness is not the running of a programme.

From a christian theological perspective, the human being is purposefully created in the image of God, which means that the

[7] Fergus Gordon Kerr, *Theology after Wittgenstein* (Oxford: Basil Blackwell, 1986), 185. As Kerr says, "the internal states of information-processing machines have become the paradigm for the psychological states of creatures of our kind" (183).

human being is created to know, worship, and glorify God. This implies that apart from the human capacity for rational thought, belief is yet another criterion of what it means to be human.

John Searle has broached this question from two vantage points.[8] Firstly, he argues that since computers are made of silicon chips and not neurons and that neurons are necessary for belief, this suggests that a computer cannot behave and function like a human being. The fact that a computer can stimulate intelligent behavior, which is characteristically a feature of brains, suggests that intelligent behavior can be carried out without a brain. This point has been raised by AI adherents against Searle's 'brain chauvinism.'

However, Searle relates this first point with his second argument, which is that there is a distinction between genuine belief and stimulated belief. Genuine belief is referred to by Searle as an 'intrinsic intentionality', which is about something or directed towards something, a contrast to an 'as-if' intentionality. The belief here is seen to be in the eye of the beholder, therefore it is not genuine belief. In Searle's view, the fact that the computer is run through a manipulation of symbols in accordance with rules is sufficient proof that it does not possess intrinsic intentionality and genuine belief.

Underlying this is a genuine concern that we may trace a certain reluctance to take our bodiliness seriously. Until such time as computer hardware can resemble the human body, it takes minimal sense to speak of minds alone. As Fergus Kerr reminds us, "the bodiliness that seems to keep us apart is exactly what makes our being together possible in the first place."[9] It is this "rancour against the physical and historical condition of human life" that creation-centered non-dualist theology makes it most valuable contribution.[10]

---

[8] John Rogers Searle, "Minds, Brains and Programs," in *Artificial Intelligence* (ed. Rainer Born; London: Croom Helm, 1987).

[9] Kerr, *Theology after Wittgenstein*, 188.

[10] Kerr, *Theology after Wittgenstein*, 188.

Mind-Body Dualism: A Theological Critique

As with the scientific revolution of the 17th and 18th centuries, Descartes' radical dissociation of the 'mind' from the 'body' and the subsequent exaltation of 'reason' over 'emotion' further reinforced the view of women and nature as objects for male use and pleasure. Feminists and ecologists, such as Lynn White, have argued that the separation of 'mind' from the 'body' is to be seen as directly responsible for the subjugation and oppression of women and for the environmental crisis. This is because, as Marti Kheel rightly contends, dualism has two characteristics in common: the first half of the duality is always valued more than the other; and, the more valued half is always seen as 'male' and the less valued half as 'female.'[11] Christian ecofeminists like Sallie McFague focus more on the inadequacies of Platonic and Enlightenment dualism for rendering a relational theology of nature.[12]

Rosemary Ruether and McFague argue that, due to the way in which dualism has functioned in creating binary oppositions, such as body/mind, male/female, and reason/emotion, it is necessary for the sake of integration and unity that we use relational language in our theological discourse, beginning, of course, with body-mind dualism. Ruether for example, argues that feminism needs to develop an anthropology which rejects traditional male definitions of certain physic attributes as being 'masculine' and 'feminine,' referring here to the reason-emotion dichotomy. As she states, "there is no biological connection between male gonads and the capacity to reason," nor there is any "biological connection between female sexual organs and the capacity to be intuitive;" "all humans possess a full and equivalent human nature and personhood, as *male and female*...since obviously males and females possess both side of the brain" [emphasis original].[13] It shows that there is no biological basis

[11] Marti Kheel, "The Liberation of Nature: A Circular Affair, Environmental Ethics," *Sociological Abstract* 7/2 (1985), 136.

[12] Sallie McFague, *The Body of God: An Ecological Theology* (London: SCM, 1993), 33.

[13] Rosemary Radford Ruether, *Gaia and God: An Ecofeminist Theology of Earth Healing* (London: SCM, 1992), 113.

for differentiating males and females into different physic profiles, but rather both sexes have the capacity for physic wholeness.

But, the recent studies regarding transvestites and sexual identity call into question Reuther's argument that due to socialization, males have developed their "left-and right-brain" capacities, while women have developed their "right-and left-brain" capacities. The studies point to the fact that in those individuals born and socialized as male or female, yet who within their innermost being felt trapped in the wrong body, there was tremendous inner turmoil until such time that they could change their sex/gender role.

Furthermore, in an age when we can transplant organs from one person to another in order to maintain life; when people's bodies can be augmented by artificial means; when person's sex can be altered; when individual can be cloned; when heterosexual and patriarchal understandings of the body are breaking down, issues of bodily identity worry us and yet in an age when aesthetics appears to have largely replaced metaphysics, the body seems to be all we have.

Maurice Merleau-Ponty and Dynamic Non-dualism

The writings of the famous phenomenologist Maurice Merleau-Ponty have been recognized by many in the last two decades as providing alternatives to a Cartesian-dualist and Enlightenment-subjectivity world view. Merleau-Ponty's writings illuminate ordinary human experience through an examination of the extraordinary-traumatic experience. According to Merleau-Ponty, human experience is a whole, not dual ('mind' and 'body'). And as a whole, it unites mind–body–world while maintaining singularity and plurality. It unites them in a story that uses the language of 'intention', 'motivation', 'direction', 'desire', 'sexuality', 'expression', and 'thought' to describe intertwining human behaviors. It dynamically unites—or tries to—traditional dichotomies of 'mind' and 'body', 'interiority' and 'exteriority', and 'subject' and 'object.' What becomes visible is corporeity existing as communication.

In the *Phenomenology of Perception*,[14] Merleau-Ponty appeals to the case studies of brain-injured men, and amputees of World War I—survivors of 'physical' and 'psychological' trauma.[15] By examining the physiological and psychic phenomena that arise in the aftermath of traumatic experience, Merleau-Ponty magnifies human corporeality as a directed self-showing. For Merleau-Ponty, trauma operates like a prism through which the body as it is experienced, lights up. Merleau-Ponty explores three kinds of bodily adaptations: anatomical, technical and verbal—as expressions of preconscious bodily desire and especially of that which is arguably a human being's most intense kind of preconscious desire—that generated by traumatic experience.

By *anatomical* adaptation, Merleau-Ponty means the spontaneous mobilizing of an organism's body cells, tissue and organs, in response to preconscious felt needs. In paralysis from spinal cord injury, the anatomical body marshals a complex set of internal adjustments to strike an equilibrium with its new circumstances. Skin adaptation is another example of anatomical shifting. Unremitting pressure on muscle and skin tissue cuts of blood circulation to the tissue and tissue dies. People with healthy spinal cords spontaneously shift their sleeping and sitting positions countless times during a day, in part because their bodies are responding to felt needs of which they are generally unaware.

If anatomical adaptation participates in life to attain new meanings , the same can be said of technical adaptation. By *technological* adaptation, Merleau-Ponty means a dually reflective and bodily process. Our body depends on technology to accommodate bodily needs that are not or cannot be met by anatomical shifting. Walking frames, hearing-aids, wheelchairs, and other assistive technologies are used to adapt to the bodily needs. Important here is the way that corporeal responsiveness reveals anatomical and technological adaptations to exist as communication. If anatomical shifting returns

---

[14] Maurice Merleau-Ponty, *Phenomenology of Perception* (trans. Colin Smith; London: Routledge & Kegan Paul, 1962 [1945]).

[15] Although Merleau-Ponty indicates the exceptional status of trauma for his project, he does not explicitly explore, specify, or reveal his implied concept of trauma.

communication to physiology, technological adaptation extends bodies beyond physiology. It shows how one's self-designating self-showing adapts to include the technologically appended lived body.

Anatomical and technological adaptation show themselves as two of the many processes through which human corporeality signifies both itself and a beyond-self; for Merleau-Ponty, a third such process is 'speech' (*verbal* adaptation). By 'speech' Merleau-Ponty means spoken or written languages that accomplish through words, thought. The *Phenomenology of perception* makes explicit the body as the basis of speech. Speech, like anatomy and technology, shows itself as signification of and intention towards expressing bodily desire to demarcate and signify self and other. For Merleau-Ponty, speech is not only inseparable from corporeity but emerging from and existing as corporeity, especially of and as desire.

In short, for Merleau-Ponty, trauma operates as a magnifying extreme that makes visible, dynamic adaptations of our verbal, anatomical, and technological bodily processes. These processes show lived body as an intended self-showing rooted in and displaying bodily desire. Finally, that each of the explored bodily processes (speech, anatomy, and assistive technology) participate in a shared aim of self and other designation, also underlines Merleau-Ponty's view of human experience as a dynamic whole, which suggests the experience of self and world as non-dual.

Alternative/Embodied Anthropology

One of the primary aims of a theological/non-dualistic critique of 'mind-body dualism' is to construct an alternative anthropology, a new understanding of human nature, that recognises the centrality of embodiment/body. Dermot Lane identifies the following steps to construct an embodied anthropology:[16]

- We must accept the relational self, "indeed, it must be said that relationality is a primary category, a fundamental characteristic of all beings in the world and not just human

[16] Dermot Lane, "Anthropology and Eschatology," *Irish Theological Quarterly* 61 (1995), 14–31.

beings."[17] It is out of this relationality that individuality emerges and that individuality can only be maintained through continuous relationality.

- We must recognize that "human beings belong to each other in an extraordinary degree of natural solidarity and social togetherness ... [which] can be seen not only at the human level but also on a wider cosmic scale in the light of the emerging creation story."[18]
- We must take the cosmic nature of human embodiment on board in our task of constructing a new anthropology. Postmodern science has taught us that all bodies—cosmic, animal and human—have an effect upon another and that effect can reach across space and time.[19]
- We must recognize the social and communal nature of human beings. Lane argues that such an alternative anthropology is fundamentally eschatological.[20]

If we are going to emphasize the relational nature of the human self, the embodied nature of the self and a self that is 'social and cosmic' in origin, then questions about the realization of the universe, and communal and individual relationships with God are unavoidable. There is a need to move away from purely individual, disembodied anthropology to embodied anthropology.[21]

Conclusion

As the locus of divine revelation, 'body' is established both as a point of contact with God and as a gulf between the divine and the human, even as we touch the divine presence we lose him/her. The human experience of embodiment is complex, ambiguous and

---

[17] Lane, "Anthropology and Eschatology,"19.

[18] Lane, "Anthropology and Eschatology," 22.

[19] Brian Swimme and Thomas Berry, *The Universe Story: From the Primordial Flaring Forth to the Ecozoic Era–A Celebration of the Unfolding Universe* (New York: HarperCollins, 1992); Rupert Sheldrake, *A New Science of Life: The Hypothesis of Formative Causation* (Los Angeles: J P Tarcher, 1981).

[20] Lane, "Anthropology and Eschatology," 24, 27.

[21] Lane, "Anthropology and Eschatology," 27.

diverse. What is remarkable is that both conservatives and feminist/queer theologians are in agreement that "the flesh is the hinge of salvation."[22] This common starting point has the potential to produce the kind of creative dialogue that has recently been lacking in theological conversations. What must be guarded against at all costs is the disappearance of the real, lived, birthing, suffering, dying, and resurrecting body underneath the philosophical and theological discourses it is called to bear.

[22] Tertullian, *De resurrection carnis*, 8.6–12.